WEST YORKSHIRE CINEMAS AND THEATRES

Picture Palace
The Picture Palace, at
Moorthorpe, opened *c.* 1912.

New Victoria/Gaumont/Odeon Twins, Prince's Way, Bradford
Photograph from the Tony Moss Collection and reproduced courtesy of the Cinema Theatre
Association.

WEST YORKSHIRE CINEMAS AND THEATRES

FEATURING IMAGES FROM THE **YORKSHIRE POST**

PETER TUFFREY

FONTHILL

The Empire Leeds,
photographed on
25 February 1961.

FONTHILL MEDIA
www.fonthill.media

Typeset in 10.5pt on 13pt Sabon LT Std
Typesetting by Fonthill Media
Printed in the UK

ISBN 978-1-78155-206-3

Contents

Acknowledgements

I am grateful for the help received from the following people: Kenny Allen, Humphrey Bolton, Paul Bolton, David Clay, Norman Ellis, Gerald England, Allan Hollings, Nigel Homer, Alexander Kapp, Matthew Lloyd, Betty Longbottom, Tony Martin, Hugh Parkin, Clive Polden, Andrew Riley, Colin Sutton, Robert Wade, Barry Watchorn, Frank Woolrych.

Special thanks are due to my son Tristram for his help and encouragement throughout the project.

Photographs
Every effort has been made to gain permission to use the photographs in this book. If you feel you have not been contacted please let me know: petertuffrey@rocketmail.com

Information
I have taken reasonable steps to verify the accuracy of the information in this book but it may contain errors or omissions. Any information that may be of assistance to rectify any problems will be gratefully received. Please contact me in writing: Peter Tuffrey, 8 Wrightson Avenue, Warmsworth, Doncaster, South Yorkshire, DN4 9QL.

Yorkshire Post
Unless otherwise stated, all photographs are copyright of *Yorkshire Post Newspapers*. View and buy these pictures by visiting www.yorkshirepost.co.uk or contact the *Yorkshire Post's* sales department on 0113 238 8360, giving the page number and full details of the picture.

Introduction

To me, it's slightly upsetting when looking at old surviving cinema buildings. For the most part they have become ugly, disfigured structures in a street or landscape. The massive, impressive buildings with fine architectural details, that were built at the height of the cinema era – during the first three decades of the twentieth century – struggle to find an alternative use. And, unfortunately they, to my mind, are the ones that stick out the most. Yet, who at that time could have predicted that 'going to the flicks', a craze that swept the world, would be rapidly superseded by television.

In a way, a comparison may be made with railway stations, particularly those which served branch lines. Numerous examples were quickly made redundant by the introduction of motorised transport. Countless railway stations and cinemas/theatres only had a comparatively short lifespan when compared with other buildings, and it is absorbing to look back at them in their prime. So having produced a book, *West Yorkshire Railway Stations*, I am pleased to offer this present book on *West Yorkshire Cinemas and Theatres*.

For the most part, the showing of films in the main areas of West Yorkshire followed a pattern that was mirrored nationally. They were largely introduced in theatres or music halls during the 1890s as part of a live entertainment programme. The growth of the industry during the first decade of the twentieth century led in many cases to theatres switching to films full time, although some continued with variety.

In West Yorkshire, where industry was rampant, there was a great need for entertainment. Therefore, it was only natural that the new film industry should spawn purpose-built cinemas across the entire West Yorkshire area. Small limited companies were established by local entrepreneurs to run these, and local architects found much work.

As the 'talkies' arrived, mostly during the late 1920s and early 1930s, many cinemas underwent refurbishment to accommodate the new equipment and provide patrons with as much comfort as possible. This also sparked a desire to build new, colossal super cinemas in a second wave of cinema building. Many of these could seat over 2,000, whereas those built in the first wave accommodated on average around 900.

In a period where health and safety was almost non-existent, it is pleasing to recall that no major loss of life occurred in the region's cinemas or theatres. That is apart from several incidents like the one at the Scala Cinema in Bradford, and not forgetting that quite a number of cinemas and theatres suffered fire damage.

Although theatre-going declined with the coming of the cinema craze, I am pleased to mention that live theatre is still very much alive across the whole region. It is particularly evident in Leeds at the West Yorkshire Playhouse, at Wakefield in the Theatre Royal and Opera House and Keighley at the Keighley Playhouse to mention just a few.

Many cinemas and theatres in the late 1950s and early 1960s started introducing bingo part-time, and then full-time. Sometimes this was a success, but not many survive as bingo venues today and demolition took place. A small number of cinemas have found other uses, but conjuring up a use for a large cavernous building with all the attendant maintenance and safety issues has been a major problem and continues to be so for those still hanging on to survival. Fortunately, a few have gained listing status, to remind us of the former great days of the cinema and theatre.

I am grateful to Peter Charlton, Editor of the Yorkshire Post Newspapers, for allowing me to use, as a basis for the book, pictures from the newspaper's archive. Gratitude should also be expressed to David Clay who trawled through the digital collection for images to use. Paul Bolton and Susan Tyler-Stringer at the YP gave additional encouragement. I am further in debt to the Tony Moss Collection held by the Cinema and Theatre Association and to Clive Polden for providing excellent scans of the images.

The significant number of images placed in the public domain on Geograph by talented and generous photographers has proved invaluable, particularly when I needed to show the cinemas as they are now. Finally, I would like to thank the late Colin Sutton, who has produced a masterly website on the history of Bradford cinemas, for his help and encouragement during the early stages of this book.

Bradford City Centre

Alhambra Theatre, Morley Street
An earlier Alhambra had opened in Canal Road in 1873 and, under William Morgan, became the Alhambra Music Hall. But the venture was short-lived as closure came two years later. The new Alhambra was designed by Leeds architects Chadwick & Watson, in a style they described as 'English renaissance of the Georgian period.' The general contractor was J. T. Wright. The theatre was opened, at a cost of £20,000, at 2 p.m. on Wednesday 18 March 1914 by Annie Laidler, wife of Francis Laidler the man behind the project. In Peter Holdsworth's book *Domes of Delight* (1989) it is stated: 'The word Alhambra is derived from the Arabic Kal'– at al hambra, which means the red castle, although Laidler's new theatre may have owed something in inspiration to the great citadel and palace built by the Moorish Kings of the 13th Century, a greater influence in practical terms was the Alhambra Theatre and Music Hall in London's Leicester Square...' The theatre opened to the general public at 6.30 p.m. on Monday 23 March 1914. The auditorium comprised orchestra stalls and pit stalls on the ground floor, dress circle and eight boxes on the first tier and a large balcony on the second tier, providing a total seating of approx 1,800, later reduced to 1,650. The picture dates from June 1957.

Bradford Picture House/Picture House/Majestic, Morley Street

The cinema opened on Thursday 2 April 1914 with the Lord Mayor of Bradford, Alderman J. Arnold officiating at the ceremony. Seating was for 1,208 patrons and the main film screened was *Spartacus – the Revolt of the Gladiators*. Ten years later the cinema's name was changed to Picture House and initial closure came on Saturday 27 October 1956. A year later the building re-opened as the Majestic Ballroom lasting until 1961 when it became a Top Rank bingo Club. A further change occurred in 1970 when it operated under the title Majestic Cinema showing Asian films. Amongst the operators were Bradford Cinematograph Co., New Century Pictures and Gaumont. Later it was used by the Alhambra as a rehearsal space.

Alhambra Theatre, Morley Street

When Francis Laidler died in 1955 his widow, Gwladys Stanley took control but the Alhambra eventually passed to Rowland Hill. In 1964 Bradford City Council bought the building for £78,900. Ten years later it was designated a Grade II Listed building. After extensive refurbishment in 1986, it re-opened on 27 May of that year. The building presently has a seating capacity of around 1,400. The photograph shows the refurbished stage area and was taken on 22 May 1986.

Cannon, Leeds Road
The Cannon originally opened as the Ritz (later becoming known as the ABC) at 7.00 p.m. on Monday 8 May 1939. The building was renamed Cannon on 10 February 1987 but closed on Thursday 17 September 1987. The last films were: Screen 1, the local premiere of *Rita, Sue and Bob Too*; Screen 2, *Hell Raiser* and Screen 3, *Lethal Weapon*. The premises were demolished in March 1988. Photograph reproduced courtesy of The Cinema Theatre Association.

Cinecenta & Penthouse Cine Club, Cheapside
The Cinecenta & Penthouse Cine Club was opened as a twin cinema by the Cinecenta chain on 17 April, 1969. The Cinecenta's first main feature was *Charlie Bubbles* starring Albert Finney and seating was provided for 260. The Penthouse Cine Club (a members-only cinema), seating 190, opened with the Swedish film *I, A Woman*. The Star Cinemas chain took over in September in 1979 but their tenure was short lived as both cinemas were closed on 7 September 1983. The Cinecenta finished with *Nathallie* and *Hot Tee Shirts* and the Penthouse Cine Club screening *Take Me In* and *Pleasure Cruise*. Photograph reproduced courtesy of The Cinema Theatre Association.

Grange Picture Theatre/the Grange, Great Horton Road
The stone-built cinema opened on Saturday 23 December 1922 when the opening film was *The Love Flower*. Seating was provided for 1,100 people and a British Thompson Houston (BTH) sound system was introduced in 1929. Then, during the early 1950s a Western Electric sound system was installed along with CinemaScope in 1954. Closure followed the screening of *The Miracle* on Saturday 15 July 1961. Later the premises were converted for commercial use: first by the Great Horton Co-op and then by a DIY firm. Photograph from the Tony Moss Collection and reproduced courtesy of The Cinema Theatre Association.

Hippodrome/Roxy, Barkerend Road
The cinema building had started life as a skating rink which opened in 1909. It was subsequently converted into a cinema by controllers the MacNaghten Vaudeville Circuit and opened on Monday 20 February 1911. Seating was initially for 1,700 (later 1,460 and then 1,373). For a time Variety was also included at the Hippodrome but this ceased in 1921. The cinema changed its name to Roxy in around 1950. In 1952 the Roxy became part of the Star Cinema chain who, two years later, added a new wide panoramic screen and this was later adapted for CinemaScope. Closure came on Wednesday 8 November 1961. The last films shown were *The Absent Minded Professor* and *The Horsemasters*. The next day, the building re-opened as the Silver Dollar Bingo Club. Later, it became an EMI Bingo & Social Club and was converted to a mosque in 1982. Photograph from the Tony Moss Collection and reproduced courtesy of The Cinema Theatre Association.

New Victoria/Gaumont/Odeon Twins, Prince's Way

The purpose-built cinema, designed by local architect Wm Illingworth for backers Provincial Cinematograph Theatres and Gaumont British Picture Corporation, was opened at 2.30 p.m. on Monday 22 September 1930. The opening ceremony was performed by the Lord Mayor of Bradford Alderman Angus Rhodes and there was a stage and film programme. Seating was planned for 3,500 but reduced to 3,318, and the building also included a café and ballroom. The proscenium was 50 feet wide and 35 feet high with a theatre stage 70 feet wide and 45 feet deep and complete with 10 dressing rooms. Thus, for many years, beside showing films the New Victoria was noted for presenting numerous stage shows. The cinema also boasted a 3-manual 10-rank Style 220 Wurlitzer pipe organ.

New Victoria/Gaumont/Odeon Twins, Prince's Way

The New Vic as it was known became the Gaumont in September 1950 and four years later CinemaScope was added. Many pop groups played at the Gaumont in the 1960s including the Rolling Stones in 1963 and 1965 and the Beatles twice in 1963 and again in 1964. The Gaumont closed on 30 November 1968 and the final film was *Rio Conchos* starring Richard Boone, Stuart Whitman and Anthony Franciosa. The building then re-opened on 21 August 1969 as Odeon Twins with the former stalls area being converted into the Top Rank Bingo Club. Odeon 3 opened on Thursday 23 June 1988. The last film to be shown was *Chicken Run* in Odeon 2 on Sunday 2 July 2000.

Odeon Cinema, Manchester Road

Architect R. Bullivant, designed the Odeon for Odeon Theatres Ltd and it opened on 17 December 1938. The main feature was *The Ware Case* which had its world premiere there. The proscenium was 38 feet wide and 14 feet deep and seating was available for 2,713 patrons. Bomb damage caused the cinema to close between 31 August and 11 November 1940. The cinema (along with the *Odeon Theatres Ltd*) was taken over by the J. Arthur Rank organisation. CinemaScope was installed during 1954 and structural alterations were carried out in 1961; the seating was also reduced to 2,447. Bradford Council acquired the Odeon leasehold in 1966 as the site was required for future city redevelopments. Thus, closure came on Saturday 22 March 1969 after the screening of *The Thomas Crown Affair*. A year later the building was demolished and the new Law Courts were erected on the site. Photograph from the Tony Moss Collection and reproduced courtesy of The Cinema Theatre Association.

Picture House/Tatler/New Tatler, Town Hall Square

The cinema, often known as the Town Hall Square Picture House, was opened in a converted warehouse by John Goodman at 7.30 p.m. on Monday 23 December 1912. The first film shown was *A Heart of Stone* and seating was available for around 700. During the silent era there was an accompaniment by a small orchestra. A Hughes Two Manual piped organ was installed in 1920 and by the end of the decade a Western Electric Sound system was added. Amongst the subsequent owners were Cinema Forum (Bradford) Ltd and Regal Cinemas (Warrington) Ltd. The name was changed to Tatler in 1931 and New Tatler in 1935 after extensive renovations and redecoration. The work included the installation of an updated Western Electric sound system and the seating being reduced to 650. The cinema closed after fire damage on Wednesday 12th December 1945. The last films shown were *Captain Blood* and *Night of Adventure*. In time, the building was used by several retailers but was demolished in the 1960s.

Picturedrome/Astra, Bridge Street
The Picturedrome was established by Victor Hamilton in the Bridge Street Wesleyan Association Chapel, dating from 1838. The venue opened on Monday 21 March, 1910 with stage acts and a film programme the latter including *An Outlaw's Sacrifice*, *The Forgotten Watch*, *Cook Makes Madeira Sauce*, and *His Only Child*. Seating was for 700 people and, for a time, variety continued to be a feature of the entertainment programme. Around 1929 a British Talking Pictures (BTP) sound system was added. Amongst the later owners were Elite Picture House Co. Ltd and Bridge Street Cinema Co. Ltd. Closure for two months, from Saturday 5 February 1949, resulted in the building being refurbished, the sound system upgraded, seating reduced to 670 and the name changed to Astra. Closure came on Sunday 29 January 1956 after the showing of *Japanese War Bride* and *Smart Boys*. The building was demolished in 1959 for road widening in the area.

Prince's Theatre, St John's Street/Little Horton Lane/Star Theatre and Music Hall, Manchester Road
Designed by Samuel Jackson and William Longley, the building was a unique two-tier construction; the lower part was initially the Star Music Hall and the upper part, the Prince's Theatre. The Star Music Hall, accommodating 2,100, opened on Monday 23 August 1875, the Prince's Theatre on 17 April, 1876. On Tuesday 16 July 1878 much of the theatre was destroyed by fire but it re-opened on Christmas Eve Wednesday 24 December 1879 with a pantomime, *Ye Fair One with the Golden Locks*. The new lessee at the time of the re-opening was Alfred Davis who in turn gave way to a Mr Sinclair, followed by a Mr Sergenson and Charles Pullan. Later owners included Walter Reynolds, from 1896, and he leased it to Francis Laidler the builder of the Alhambra. Finally, closure came on Saturday 27 May 1961 and the building was demolished in 1964.

Regent/Essoldo, Manningham Lane

There was a civic opening of the cinema at 5.00 p.m. on Wednesday 30 September 1914 and it was attended by the Lord Mayor of Bradford Alderman J. Arnold. The plans for the building were produced by local architect H. W. Rogerson for the owner, master photographer William Frederick George Phillips. The splendid frontage in white terracotta was in the French Classic style and the building was topped by an octagonal tower and dome. Seating was provided for 1,377 patrons. The building also included a café, a proscenium opening 30 feet wide and a stage with two dressing rooms. The Regent opened with a concert programme and the first film was shown to the public on Friday 2 October 1914: *The Opera Singers Triumph*. A highlight came on Monday 29 November 1920 at 2.45 p.m. when HRH Duke of York attended a matinée performance. For a time in the mid-1920s the building operated as the Regent Theatre but afterwards and following some renovation it re-opened as the New Regent with new owners. An RCA Sound System was installed in 1929 but later a Western Electric's Mirrophonic Sound System was added. Subsequent controllers included the Emery Cinema Circuit Ltd and Sol Sheckman's Essoldo Circuit. The cinema's name was changed to Essoldo in 1950 and included in further extensive alterations in 1954 was the introduction of CinemaScope. Closure came on Saturday 30 October 1965 after the showing of *Dual at Rio Bravo* and *Monster from an Unknown World*. In time the building reopened as the Lucky Seven Bingo Club & Casino but was later run by the Pakistan National Film Club. Following a disastrous fire on Wednesday 25 February 1976 the building was eventually demolished. The photograph was taken in the aftermath of the fire.

Ritz/ABC, Broadway/Leeds Road

Designed by architect W. R. Glen for owner John Maxwell's ABC (Associated British Cinemas) the Ritz (later becoming known as the ABC) opened at 7.00 p.m. on Monday 8 May 1939. There was a spectacular gala opening ceremony which was attended by the Lord Mayor of Bradford Alderman T. J. Robinson and John Maxwell himself. The first film shown was *The Citadel*. A cream terracotta faience was a feature of the exterior building which also incorporated several self-contained shop units. Seating was for 2,037 customers. The proscenium opening was 38 feet wide, the stage 15 feet deep, and there were two dressing rooms. A 3-manual Compton organ was also installed. Both photographs from the Tony Moss Collection and reproduced courtesy of The Cinema Theatre Association.

Ritz/ABC, Broadway/Leeds Road

On Friday 20 September 1946 heavy storms caused flood damage to the Ritz and it was closed for almost a week. A panoramic wide screen was added in 1953, 3-D and CinemaScope a year later. During the 1960s an RCA sound set was added and from February 1969 EMI took control. The building opened as a 'Triple' on 18 November 1974 and became known as the ABC Film Centre. Seating in the three areas was now: ABC 1,732; ABC 2, 184 and ABC 3 166. In February 1987 control passed to Cannon but the cinema closed on Thursday 17 September 1987. The closing film in ABC1 was the premiere of *Rita, Sue and Bob Too*. In March of the following year the building was demolished. Photograph from the Tony Moss Collection and reproduced courtesy of The Cinema Theatre Association.

St George's Hall, Hall Ings

St George's Hall was built as a concert hall and officially opened on 29 August 1853 by HRH Queen Victoria and HRH Prince Albert. Originally the seating capacity was for 3,500 people. Films were shown at the Hall irregularly from 1898 until the building opened properly as a cinema on Thursday 1 April 1926 and was initially operated by New Century Pictures. The seating capacity was 2,116 and the first film shown was *The Eagle*. The cinema closed on Saturday 12 March 1949 after the showing of *Deep Waters* and *Pin Up Girl*. Then, the building was acquired by Bradford Council and modernised for use as a concert hall, re-opening on 30 September 1953.

Savoy, Darley Street
The building was designed by Moore & Crabtree of whom E. G. Moore was the proprietor. Opening on Monday 29 March 1920, the first film shown was *The Canadian Tour*. There were seats for 1,593 patrons and this included the stalls, circle and gallery. In 1927 a 2-manual 8-rank Jardine Orchestral Organ was installed. On 9 March 1929 the cinema showed the first full-length all-talkie film in Bradford – *The Singing Fool*. Amongst the subsequent owners were Savoy Cinemas Ltd, and ABC (Associated British Cinemas). The Savoy underwent alterations in 1932 but four years later, on 18 January 1936, it was the scene of an explosion which occurred in the projection room. Several people were injured and the cinema closed for just over two weeks. Final closure came on Saturday 15 April, 1939 after the showing of *Mysterious Mr Moto* and *Hold My Hand*. The site was acquired by Marks & Spencer and subsequently redeveloped. Photograph from the Tony Moss Collection and reproduced courtesy of The Cinema Theatre Association.

Scala Picture House, East Parade
The first films shown were *Deerslayer* and *The Test* on 2 August 1913. The cinema was a purpose-built, three-storey, stone building designed by Ed. Simpson & Son and seating was provided for 700 people. The proprietors were the Tivoli Picture Hall Company and the Catholic Church. A pianist provided a Musical accompaniment for the silent films. An alarming accident occurred on New Year's Day 1916 when a strong gale dislodged a stone cross on the gable end of the adjacent St Mary's Roman Catholic Church, which fell through the Scala roof. Albert E. Rawse, aged 12, was killed and at least two more badly injured. The cinema closed in 1922. Three years later it re-opened as Concert Party Theatre but this was short-lived. A year on and it became St Mary's Church Hall, then the St Mary's Centre. Copyright photograph reproduced courtesy of Betty Longbottom.

Temperance Hall/Film Theatre, Chapel Street

The Temperance Hall was built in 1837 and could accommodate around 600. Films were shown there from 1900 and on a more regular basis from 1908 under Sidney Prince's guidance. In 1909 it closed for alterations to meet safety requirements and re-opened as a dedicated cinema on Wednesday 22 September of the latter year. Further alterations and a change of controller occurred in February 1910 when Henry Hibbert came to the fore. However, the venture was short-lived and closure came on 25 March 1922, with the showing of *His Friend's Wife* and *No Man's Land*. A little later, the building re-opened as the Jowett Hall, named after Fred Jowett who was very active in the Bradford Independent Labour Party (ILP). On 25 March 1935 the Jowett Hall was destroyed by fire. But almost two years later, on 29 January 1937 the Civic Playhouse and Film theatre was built on the old site. The bottom photograph, taken on Saturday 28 January 1911, is from the Tony Moss Collection and reproduced courtesy of The Cinema Theatre Association. The one above was taken on 4 December 1991.

Tennyson Cinema, Tennyson Place, Otley Road
The purpose-built brick cinema opened at 6.30 p.m., on Saturday 13th October 1923 showing *Moran of the Mary Letty* and *The Japanese Earthquake*. The proprietor was Albert Shackleton and seating was available for 1,166 (885 in the stalls and 277 in the balcony). By the end of the decade a Western Electric sound system had been added. Amongst the later owners were Lyceum Cinema Company and Hibbert's Pictures Ltd. During the 1950s CinemaScope was installed and the seating capacity reduced from 1,157 (which occurred in the early 1940s) to 1,095 seats. Closure came after the showing of *G.I. Blues* on Saturday 1 July 1961. In time, the building re-opened as Tennyson Bingo and Social Club but was eventually demolished. Photograph from the Tony Moss Collection and reproduced courtesy of The Cinema Theatre Association.

Theatre Royal Picture House/Irving Royal/Classic, Manningham Lane
Originally titled Alexandra Theatre, the building was designed by local architects Andrews & Son & Pepper for J. B. Buckstone and Wilde. It was built at a cost of around £6,000 by W. Morgan and opened on 26 December 1864. Seating was available for around 1,800 people (200, Dress Boxes; 250, Upper Boxes; 600 in the Pit, and 750 in the Gallery. Photograph reproduced courtesy of Matthew Lloyd.

Theatre Royal Picture House/Irving Royal/Classic, Manningham Lane

The building was later renamed the Theatre Royal and was showing films by the 1890s as part of its entertainment programme. It became a dedicated cinema on Monday 5 December 1921. The opening ceremony was performed by the Lord and Lady Mayoress of Bradford, Mr and Mrs T. Blythe. The event was marked by a double feature film programme which included *The Idle Class* and *The Quest of Happiness*. There were 1,350 seats. A 2-manual Andrews organ was installed in 1922. Subsequent owners of the premises included Expo 20 Ltd and Classic Cinemas. The building re-opened as Irving Royal on 27 February 1967, then in October of the same year, the name was changed to Classic Cinema. *The Graduate* and *Midnight Cowboy* were the last films shown on Saturday 16 November 1974. After being used as a furniture store the building was demolished *c.* 1990. Both photographs are from the Tony Moss Collection and reproduced courtesy of The Cinema Theatre Association.

Above: **Tivoli Picture Hall, Leeds Road**
The cinema was opened by Joseph McFarlane's Tivoli Picture House Co. Ltd in a stone building on Monday 23 September, 1912. Accommodation was provided for 536 people. The opening programme included the showing of the following: *Rivals, The Governor, Two Men and the Law, Road Agent's Love, His Mother-in-Law*. Seating in the 1930s was reduced to 500 and amongst the subsequent owners were Rev B. McAdam and Flanagan's Tivoli (Leeds Road) Ltd. A double feature, *Fighter Attack* and *The Harassed Hero* ended life for the cinema on Saturday 24 February 1956. Afterwards the building housed motor car showrooms and in turn a mini-market. Photograph from the Tony Moss Collection and reproduced courtesy of The Cinema Theatre Association.

Bradford District

Bingley – Hippodrome, Main Street

The cinema was opened *c.* 1914 and owned by the Bingley Hippodrome Company. It had a 26 feet wide proscenium and seated approx. 769. It was later equipped with a Western Electric sound system. Closure came *c.* 1954 and the building was subsequently used by Woolworths. The site is currently part of a car park.

Opposite below: **Towers Hall Cinema, Manchester Road**

Towers Hall was originally a skating rink and opened on Easter Monday 5 April 1909. A cinema was opened in the converted rink on Monday 25 September 1911 by Hibbert's Pictures. The opening films included *Fight With Fire*, *Battle Hymn of the Republic*, *The Outlaw Samaritan*, *Captain Kate* plus 3 comedy films. Seating was for 1,078 and initially Kine-Variety was a feature of the entertainment programme. In 1931 a British Talking Pictures sound system was added and seating capacity reduced to 996. During the 1950s a new British Thompson Houston sound system was installed along with CinemaScope in 1954 but with mono sound. The cinema closed on Saturday 21 May 1966 after showing *Thunderball*. After a period of being sublet to an Asian film society, the premises were destroyed by fire on 16 September 1970 and later demolished. Photograph from the Tony Moss Collection and reproduced courtesy of The Cinema Theatre Association.

Bankfoot – Ideal Picture House, Manchester Road

According to the *Bradford Daily Telegraph* the cinema opened on Monday 15 March 1914. Bankfoot Pictures Ltd were behind the project and their purpose-built two-storey building, costing £6,000, seated 700. Subsequent owners included James Whiteside and Cecil Barnett. Without embracing the 'talkie' era, the cinema closed on 31 March 1930 but re-opened four years later as the Ideal Ballroom. In 1962 the building housed the Ideal Bingo Club, and was then used as a warehouse and later by a carpet company. Photograph from the Tony Moss Collection and reproduced courtesy of The Cinema Theatre Association.

Dudley Hill – Dudley Hill Picture Palace, Tong Street

The cinema opened in a building designed by Cleckheaton architects Howarth & Howarth for owners Walter and Percy Goodall on 9 December 1912. A splendid white faience entrance including 'Marmo' tiles made by the Leeds Fireclay Company was a feature of the exterior design. The proscenium arch was approx. 30 feet wide with a stage depth of about 10 feet. John Theabold & Sons undertook the interior plasterwork. The premises opened with the showing of *How's Your Father* and seating was for 600 patrons. Photograph from the Tony Moss Collection and reproduced courtesy of The Cinema Theatre Association.

Dudley Hill – Dudley Hill Picture Palace, Tong Street

Talkies arrived Dudley Hill Picture Palace on Monday 27 October 1930 with screening of the first full-length film *Such Men are Dangerous*. Subsequent owners of the premises included Goodhall's Pictures (1931) and in 1956 CinemaScope was installed. Closure came on 1 April 1967 after the showing of a double feature *Thunderbirds are Go* and *Beauty and the Beast*. Afterwards the building was used for bingo but was later taken over by a carpet retailer who has retained much of the 1912 interior appearance. Both photographs are copyright and reproduced courtesy of Andrew Riley.

East Bowling – Coventry Hall Picture House, Coventry Street, Wakefield Road
Operator Albert E. Shields opened the Coventry Hall in premises, formerly owned by the Bradford Coffee Tavern Company, on Easter Saturday, 22 April 1913. The main feature was *The Dawning* starring Leah Baird, Harry Northrup and Earle Williams and the initial seating capacity was approx. 476 (*c.* 350 stalls and *c.* 126 balcony). The proscenium was 22 feet wide and the frontage of building underwent alterations in 1930. Sound systems installed included the AWH system. Amongst the subsequent proprietors were Northern Cinemas Co. Ltd, Ace Cinemas and Parman Cinemas. *Room at the Top* with Laurence Harvey, Simone Signoret and Heather Sears was the last screening on Saturday 12 December 1959. Later, the premises were demolished in the widening of Wakefield Road.

Eccleshill – Palladium/Regal, Norman Lane
A double feature programme opened the Palladium at 6.30 p.m. on Monday 7 January 1929. The films shown were *Blood Ship* and *Her Summer Hero*. Builder Ralph Dickinson was the proprietor and erected the building. Seats were available for 1,000 people. In May 1930 a British Thompson Houston sound system was operational. A name change occurred a year later when the Palladium became the Regal. Subsequent owners included John Lambert trading as Modern Theatres, Regal Eccleshill Ltd, Sidney Segalman and the Star Cinema chain. The premises were refurbished in 1958 and a widescreen and CinemaScope added, but with mono sound. Closure came on Wednesday 23 November 1966 after the screening of *Hound of the Baskervilles and The Steel Bayonet*. Thereafter, the building opened as the Regal Bingo & Social Club, then Regal Snooker Club and later Flacks Fitness. Photograph from the Tony Moss Collection and reproduced courtesy of The Cinema Theatre Association.

Eccleshill – Eccleshill Picture House later Eccleshill Picture Palace, Institute Road

A Mechanics' Institute, built in 1868, was converted by Charles Bottomley for the cinema to open on 2 October 1911. It was announced that 'A First-Class Programme of Pictures with Piano Accompaniment' would feature on the opening night and the initial seating capacity was 359. Shortly after opening the name was changed from Eccleshill Picture House to Eccleshill Picture Palace. In November 1920 D. B. Proctor's Patent Stereoscopic Screen was installed along with a mechanical organ – an Orchestrion – in 1929. Subsequent owners included Arnold Cinemas and a Mrs Bailey. Sound equipment was never installed in the cinema and closure came in 1931. The building later found use as the Eccleshill Youth & Community Centre and is still extant. Photograph from the Tony Moss Collection and reproduced courtesy of The Cinema Theatre Association.

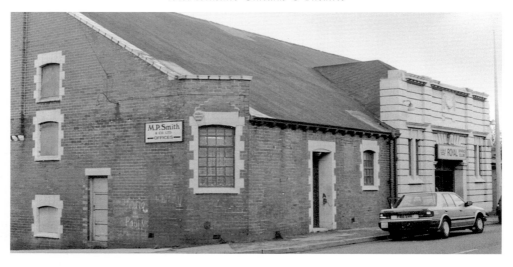

Great Horton – Cross Lane Picture House/Plaza, Cross Lane
The Cross Lane Picture House opened its doors on Monday 28 September 1914 to show *The Scales of Justice*. The proprietor was Robert Richardson, and the initial seating capacity 750. The main entrance featured a white faience façade and the proscenium was 19 feet wide. Kinema-variety was featured in the years after the First World War and in 1930 a Western Electric sound system was installed heralding the arrival of the talkies at the cinema. The building became the Plaza from Monday 10 April 1933 and with an increase in seating to 787. Amongst the later owners were West Bradford Picture Theatres and the Star Cinema chain. CinemaScope was installed in 1954 and *The Premature Burial* with Ray Milland, Hazel Court and Richard Ney was the last screening on Wednesday 20 March 1963. A month later the premises re-opened as the Lucky Diamond Bingo Club, then in 1980, following alterations, became the Royal Bingo Club. Bingo ended in 2007, and the interior of the building in recent years has been restored to its original 1914 appearance. Photograph from the Tony Moss Collection and reproduced courtesy of The Cinema Theatre Association.

Haworth – Brontë Cinema, Victoria Road
The Brontë Cinema operated between 1921 and 1956. The last film shown on 29 July of the latter year was *On the Riviera* starring Danny Kaye. Copyright photograph reproduced courtesy of Andrew Riley.

Heaton – Elite Cinema, Toller Lane

Owners, the Elite Picture House Co. Ltd opened the cinema on Friday 1 August 1913. Amongst the first films shown were: *Lord Mayor of London's Visit to Harrogate* and *The Village Blacksmith*. Seating accommodation was for 700. The premises were rebuilt and enlarged in 1924 to house 1,304 seats. It re-opened at 6.30 p.m. on Thursday 5 February, showing *Behold This Woman*. A system of synchronised sound was operational from Monday 7 January 1929. In the following decade a mixture of variety acts and films provided entertainment at the venue. Later owners included C & H (Cawthorne & Hyde) Cinemas and the Star Cinema chain. A new panoramic widescreen was installed in February 1954 and later it was adapted for CinemaScope. Closure came on Sunday 25 February 1968 after the showing of *The Yellow Teddybears* and *Beast*

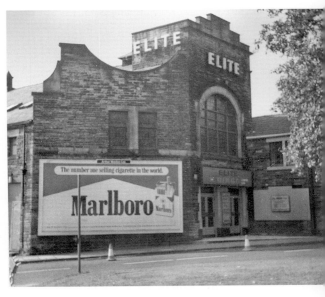

with a Million Eyes. Early in the following month the main area of the building re-opened as the Star Bingo Club but other parts were leased to Five Cities Films Ltd. Also, for a period children's film matinées were staged. In December 1986 the building was sold to Bradford's largest Moslem organisation but was partially damaged by fire in 1987 though rebuilding work took place in the 1990s. Also, the surviving frontage is a reminder of former times.

Laisterdyke – Lyceum Cinema, Bradford Lane

The cinema opened on 18 December 1919. The first film shown was *Daddy Long Legs*. Seating was for 1,112 patrons. Amongst the former owners were the Lyceum Picture House Co. (Bradford) Ltd, Lyceum Cinema Co. Ltd and Hibbert's Pictures. In 1930 an American Western Electric sound system was added. A wide screen – the first one to be used in a Bradford cinema – was installed in 1953; CinemaScope was added two years later. Closure came on Saturday 13 October 1962 after the showing of *Escape from Bahrain* and *The Durant Affair*. In the same year, the building re-opened as the Lyceum Bingo & Cabaret Club. It then became the Lyceum Rainbow Club, the Talk of Yorkshire, Broadway Bar and 147 Snooker Bar. Photograph from the Tony Moss Collection and reproduced courtesy of The Cinema Theatre Association.

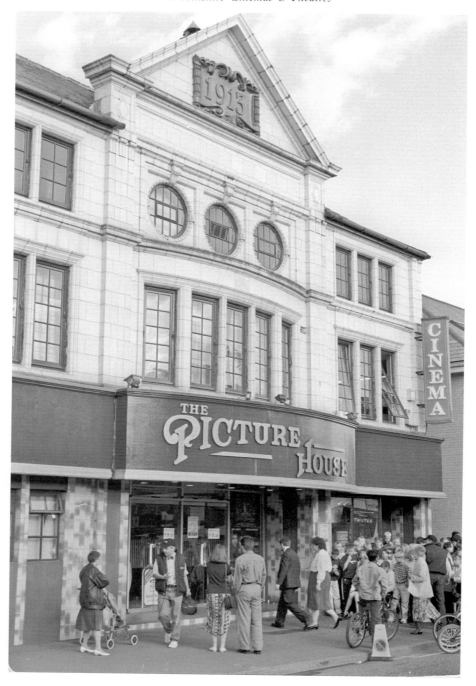

Keighley – Keighley Picture House, North Street

The Picture House opened on 10 May 1913 with seating for 866, divided between stalls and a single balcony. Initially it was run by a board of directors which included Sir Harry Smith of Dean Smith & Grace, the machine tools manufacturers. On occasions the entertainment programme featured live acts. During the 1930s The Arcadian Follies from Morecambe were a regular feature. Later, in the late 1950s and early 1960s there were one night shows starring Billy Fury, Marty Wilde and Wee Willy Harris. Later operators included Essoldo and Classic Cinemas. The building was twinned in the mid 1970s and closed in 1991. But, after extensive repairs it was re-opened in 1997, still as a twin (308 seats, screen 1; 93 screen 2), by Northern Morris Cinemas and is thriving today.

Keighley – Keighley Playhouse, Devonshire Street

Keighley Playhouse began life as an offshoot by members of Keighley Amateur Operatic and Dramatic Society, led by the late Frederick Pye, who wished to present 'straight' plays as an alternative to the amateur operatic diet of musicals and pantomimes. The early productions were staged at the Temperance Hall in Albert Street Keighley with the very first being a performance of J. B. Priestley's classic *When We Are Married*. Following a series of seven successful productions over two years, the group re-located to Devonshire Hall in Devonshire Street, Keighley where the Playhouse has now been established for over 60 years. At the time, Devonshire Hall was an unused public meeting hall and the Keighley Theatre Group, as it was then known, began presenting a regular season of six plays per annum. Over time the group was variously known as The Theatre Group, Keighley Little Theatre and eventually Keighley Playhouse. During the late 1960s and early 1970s the group experienced severe financial difficulties and was on the brink of total collapse until the appointment of F. Walter Twigg as chairman. His contribution was unquestionably why Keighley Playhouse still exists today. Keighley Playhouse currently presents seven productions each year between September and June, each production being presented for six performances. The Playhouse is a wholly amateur organisation and is managed on a day-to-day basis by a 12-strong management committee elected annually by the membership. Copyright photograph reproduced courtesy of Keighley Playhouse.

Keighley – Ritz/ABC, Alice Street
The Ritz Cinema was opened by Associated British Cinemas on 28 February 1938. The work had been started by Union Cinemas before the ABC takeover. The building was designed by Sam Beverley of Verity & Beverley and seating was for 1,526. The cinema also incorporated a café-restaurant, which accommodated 100. Shortly after being renamed ABC on 30 July 1971 closure followed on 2 February 1974. Later the building was converted to a bingo hall. The photograph was taken on 17 February 1986.

Lidget Green – Arcadian, Legrams Lane
The Arcadian was built on the site of the Arcadian Pavilion, a wooden structure, which existed between 1908 and 1931. Lord Mayor of Bradford, Alderman M. F. Titterington officiated at the Arcadian cinema's opening on Saturday 16 March 1940. Seating was for 1,000 with 680 in the stalls and 320 in the balcony. The opening film was *The Spy in Black* starring Conrad Veidt, Sebastian Shaw and Valerie Hobson. The proscenium was 38 feet wide and the stage 15 feet deep with two dressing rooms. Former operators included Shack Hyde's Glenroyal Cinema Co. Closure came on Saturday 8 February 1964 after the showing of *Jason and the Argonauts*. Thereafter the building became the Arcadian Bingo Club, and in time reverted back to being a cinema – the Commonwealth Film Club – to show Asian films. This lasted until 1986 and in the following year the building was demolished. Photograph from the Tony Moss Collection and reproduced courtesy of The Cinema Theatre Association.

Manningham – Marlboro Cinema, Carlisle Road

Designed by architect T. Patrick cinema opened
at 7.30 p.m. on Monday 28 November 1921. The
opening featured a double silent movie attraction:
Love's Harvest and *The Church on Over Shot
Wheel*. Seating was provided for 1,250 people
(1,227 in 1944 and 1,200 in the 1950s). By 1930
a British Thompson Houston sound system was
added, a Western Electric sound set was installed in
1950 along with a wide screen and CinemaScope
a little later in the decade. The Star Cinema chain
acquired the premises in 1950 and it was under
their ownership that the Marlborough closed on
Wednesday 10 October 1962 after screening two
X-certificate films *Madeleine* and *The Young Have
No Morals*. Thereafter the premises housed the
Star Bingo Club (it had been running part – time
before the cinema's closure) until 1968. Between
1968 and 1982 the building became known as the
Liberty Cinema and several groups showed films
there including Anglo-Overseas Distributors, Indo-
Pak Film Club and Asian Film Club. Then, the
building found other commercial uses but in 2000
it was transformed into the north's first dedicated

Bollywood cinema. It was opened on Friday 7 July of the latter year. Six months later on
Monday 8 January 2001, fire severely damaged the building but it was later brought back
into use as an Asian marriage and function hall. Photograph from the Tony Moss Collection
and reproduced courtesy of The Cinema Theatre Association.

Low Moor – Low Moor Picture Palace, Huddersfield Road

The cinema was established in a former single-storey Brotherhood Mission Hall by proprietors
J. B. Simpson and John Lush. It opened on Monday 14 September 1914. Seating was for 538
(later 526 and then 490) persons. The opening programme featured the latest news pictures
documenting the First World War and a serial. The talkies arrived in 1931 when a British
Thompson Houston sound system was added. Later, Austin and George Lush (John's sons) took
control of the operation. *Reap the Wild Wind* with John Wayne was shown before closure on
Saturday 15 June 1957. Seven years later the building was used by the Pelican Bingo Club until
1983. Thereafter the building has been put to other commercial uses. Copyright photograph
reproduced courtesy of Andrew Riley.

Manningham – Sangeet, Carlisle Road

The Sangeet opened in the former Manningham Methodist Church, showing Asian films, in 1970. At the rear of the building, a smaller cinema, The Naz was established but it only opened on certain occasions. The Sangeet closed in March 1980 and following a fire in 1986 the building was demolished. Photograph from the Tony Moss Collection and reproduced courtesy of The Cinema Theatre Association.

Saltaire – Saltaire Picture House/Gaumont, Bingley Road

Architect William Illingworth designed Shipley's largest cinema for owners Saltaire Picture House Ltd and it opened on the afternoon of Saturday 17 June 1922. In attendance was the Lord Mayor of Bradford, Councillor J. Blyth. There were 1,500 seats and the first film was *A Virtuous Vamp*. An orchestra was employed during the silent film era and a reed organ was also in use there. The first talkie film was shown in 1930 after a British Acoustic Sound system was added. Listed amongst the later controllers of the house were Denman Picture Houses Ltd, Gaumont British Picture Corporation, and the Rank Organisation. The cinema's name was changed to Gaumont in 1945. The following decade was marked by the installation of CinemaScope in 1955, the addition of a larger screen and the seating reduced to 1,400. *Lust for Life* was the last film shown on 19 October 1959 and the premises have been demolished.

Shipley – Glenroyal Cinema, Briggate

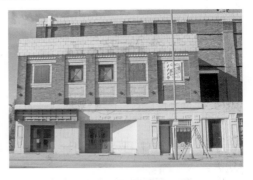

The Chairman of Shipley U.D.C. Councillor Gordon Waddilove performed the opening ceremony at the cinema, for owners the Shipley Picture House Company, at 2.30 p.m. on Monday 5 September 1932. The building was designed by Ernest Dawson – a Manchester architect. The cinema included a 30-feet wide proscenium, seating for 1,100 patrons and a Western Electric Sound System. The first film shown was *Emma* with Marie Dressler, Richard Cromwell and Myrna Loy. In the 1950s a new wide dimension screen was installed in 1953; a year later the cinema was showing 3-D films and in 1955 CinemaScope. As a cinema, the Glenroyal closed on Saturday 8 December 1962 after showing *The Loudest Whisper* and *Gun Street*. Thereafter, the Star Cinema chain converted it into the Glen Casino and in later years it became EMI Bingo & Social Club, Walkers Bingo and King's Bingo & Social Club. The latter closed on 30 January 2005 and the building was badly damaged by fire in January 2013. Copyright photograph reproduced by courtesy of Humphrey Bolton.

Shipley – Prince's Hall/Studios/Unit Four, Bradford Road

The Shipley Pavilion – a tent-type structure – existed on the site from 30 March 1907. In 1911 Bradford architect William Illingworth designed the Prince's Hall to be built on the land for owners New Century Pictures trading as Prince's Hall (Shipley) Ltd. It opened on at 2.30 p.m. Saturday 24 June 1911, having cost £6,000. In the evening there was a special programme featuring the Coronation of King George V. Seating was for approx. 1,100 patrons, the proscenium opening 22 feet in width. In the early years an orchestra accompanied the silent films and during 1920 a 2-manual Andrews pipe organ was added. By the turn of the decade an American Western Electric sound system was operational. Further developments in the 1950s included the installation of a panoramic screen in 1953 and CinemaScope a year later. Subsequent controllers included C & H Cinemas and Star Cinemas. After closure for alterations in 1972 the cinema re-opened on Sunday 13 August of that year as Studios 1-4. In 1978 the cinema changed ownership to Burnley-based Hutchinson Cinemas (Hutchinson Leisure Ltd) and was renamed Unit Four. Storm damage caused temporary closure in 1980/1981. Later, the premises were controlled by Apollo Theatres Ltd and afterwards by Marsek Ltd. In time the cinema became known as Shipley Flicks but closure came in March 2000 and the building was demolished a year later.

Skipton – Plaza, Sackville Street

The cinema's website states that the building was originally built in 1873 as a temperance hall but converted to a cinema in 1912, opening as The Gem. It was acquired in the early 1920s by Mathew Hartley & Son and stayed in the family for three generations until it was sold to the present owner, Mr Charles Morris, in May 1998 to become a Northern Morris Cinema. *The Telegraph & Argus*, on Saturday 2 May 1998 stated: ' Our favourite story from the Plaza's long history concerns the management's way of keeping rowdy youngsters in check in those long gone days. The Plaza's secret weapon was a long pole with a stuffed boxing glove on the end. Anyone who started throwing popcorn, making too much noise or any committing any other misdemeanour would get a solid poke with the boxing glove from the extra long arm of the law!' The cinema has a balcony and seating for 250 customers. A Conn 651 organ has been recently installed and there are regular organ recitals which have included well known organists such as Miss Frieda Hall and Arnold Loxam. The cinema also contains a dvd library with over 2,000 titles on display including the latest blockbuster releases. Copyright photograph reproduced courtesy of Alexander Kapp.

Skipton – Regal (formerley Morriseum)/Odeon/Classic Cinema, Keighley Road

Mark Morris, formerly associated with Skipton's Plaza, opened a new cinema, the Morriseum, on 4 February 1929. The building was designed by J. W. Broughton and included 927 seats. The first film shown was *The Spy*. The building was subsequently named Regal and then Odeon having been taken over by the latter company in 1936. In time it was controlled by Classic Cinemas and took the name Classic Cinema. Subsequent owners included the Hutchinson Circuit, Apollo Leisure Group. Closure as a cinema – the Regal – a name taken back around 1971, occurred on 10 September 1987. Later, the building became a nightclub under the titles Bliss and the Vestry and a bar, No. 3. Copyright photograph reproduced courtesy of Robert Wade.

Thornbury – Odeon Leeds, Bradford, Dick Lane, Gallagher Leisure Park
The cinema, a multiplex, located between Bradford and Leeds, opened on 6 July 2000, showing *Stuart Little*. It has 13 screens, the largest having 442 seats down to the smallest with 126 seats. During October 2011 the cinema finished the conversion to digital of all 13 screens using NEC digital cinema projectors, Doremi Servers and Unique System's Rosetta Bridge Theatre Management System. Copyright photograph reproduced courtesy of Betty Longbottom.

Undercliffe – Oxford Hall Picture Palace, Idle Road
The Oxford Hall was opened by the Undercliffe Picture House Company Ltd on 9 April 1914 with the showing of *The Adventures of Kathlyn* with Kathlyn Williams, Charles Clary and William Carpenter. There were 678 seats and a Western Electric sound system was installed around 1930. The building eventually fell under the control of Cliff Parrott's Parman Cinemas, Lionel Agar's Ace Cinemas and Threedee Ltd of Liverpool. The building was extensively refurbished in 1955 and included adding a new panoramic screen later adapted for CinemaScope. Photograph from the Tony Moss Collection and reproduced courtesy of The Cinema Theatre Association.

Undercliffe – Oxford Hall Picture Palace, Idle Road

From Thursday 13th December 1962 bingo sessions were held (under the title of Oxford Bingo and Social Club) on Thursday, Friday and Saturday evenings. Films were shown on the other days of the week. Final closure as a cinema occurred over the weekend 8 and 9 January 1966 after the showing (on the Sunday) of *Fire Over England* and *The Widow*. By the end of the month the premises were operating as the Top Flight Bingo Club. Photograph from the Tony Moss Collection and reproduced courtesy of The Cinema Theatre Association.

Wyke – Wyke Hippodrome/Star, Garden Field

The Wyke Zion Congregational Chapel was built in 1885. It was converted to a cinema by John Lambert and opened on 4 September 1926. There were 696 seats (later reduced to 580 and then 517) the proscenium opening was 20 feet wide. Closure came in 1931 and for a time the premises were used as a billiard hall. Then, after the building was re-equipped and a British Thompson Houston Sound System installed, it re-opened as a cinema on Monday 4 January 1937, showing *Ball at the Savoy* and *Seven Keys to Baldplate*. A name change to Wyke Star occurred in 1950 after a refurbishment programme; a wide screen was added in 1954. In later years the cinema was under the control of Uni-Cinemas Ltd and Pentland Hick Cinemas. A fire on Thursday 26 February 1959 caused the cinema to close. The last films screened were *Crash Landing* and *The Tall 'T'*. During subsequent years several commercial ventures have found use for the building. Copyright photograph reproduced courtesy of Humphrey Bolton.

Calderdale

Brighouse – Albert Theatre & Opera House, Huddersfield Road
Designed by the architectural firm of Sharp & Waller, the Albert Theatre & Opera House opened, at a cost of £4,000, on 30 September 1899. The Huddersfield Amateur Operatic Society put on the first stage show with a performance of *Iolanthe*. Seating was for approx. 1,098 and this included orchestra stalls, dress circle and gallery levels. Films were show intermittently until 1910 and then more regularly. A Western Electric sound system had been added by April 1930 and in the same decade the building underwent considerable alterations.

Brighouse – Albert Theatre & Opera House, Huddersfield Road

In 1953 CinemaScope was added at the Albert Theatre and amongst the later controllers included the Star Cinema chain. Closure came on 31 July 1971. In time, the building was converted for use as a bingo hall, then as the Barracuda Bar, which has been renamed The Calder. Copyright photograph reproduced courtesy of Andrew Riley.

Brighouse – Ritz Cinema, Bradford Road

The Union Cinemas chain opened the Ritz in March 1937. There were 986 seats for patrons. Later controllers included the Associated British Cinemas (ABC) chain. After closure on 24 June 1961, the building found further uses as a bingo hall, and a ballroom when a 3Manual/10Ranks Wurlitzer organ was installed. Copyright photograph reproduced courtesy of Gerald England.

Elland – Central Picture House/Rex, Coronation Street

The Rex opened as the Central Picture House on 12 December 1912. It was operated by Central Pictures (Elland) Ltd. Currently, the cinema's website states the manager and pianist was Harry Taylor. Within a few years the company had taken over the Town Hall (later the Palladium) cinema in town, which had been showing films since 1909. The two cinemas were managed by James Montgomery. The Central closed in January 1959 and the Palladium followed in June the same year.

'Walker Cinemas of Huddersfield then acquired the Central, carried out a refurbishment (including the installation of Cinemascope) and re-opened it as the Rex in November 1959. Bingo sessions were held a couple of evenings during the week in 1964 and took over completely later in the year. Proprietorship changed a couple of times and a further trial of films occurred between November 1975 and August 1977, after which bingo resumed. The enterprise folded sometime in 1985,' says the Rex website.

In 1988 the Rex was taken over by Charles Morris and Peter Berry, extensively refurbished and opened on 7 October of that year. It has since built up a reputation of a well run, comfortable but traditional cinema showing a wide range of films. Concerts on the Conn 651 organ are held on the third Sunday of each month and the organ is also played on Saturday evenings before the film and during the interval.

Halifax – Alhambra, St James Road

Built as the Oddfellows Hall in 1840, the building was initially used for concerts and entertainments. Eighteen years later Charles Dickens appeared there to give readings from *A Christmas Carol*. He didn't like Halifax much: 'It is as horrible a place as I ever saw, I think.' By 1888 the building was converted into a music hall becoming known as Halifax Peoples' Palace and eventually controlled by the MacNaghten Vaudeville Circuit. Films were introduced just after the First World War by Lewis Wormold, who leased the premises from the Halifax Friendly & Trades Society. The building became known as the Alhambra Picture House, and eventually, Alhambra Cinema. The entrance in Victoria Street down the side of the building can be seen in the photograph. Although acquired by Halifax Council in 1955, it continued to show films with a 20-foot screen in a 25-foot-wide proscenium. Closure came on 20 June 1959 and the building was demolished just over four years later. Photograph reproduced courtesy of Tony Martin.

Cosy Cinema (also known as The Cosy Corner Picture Palace or just the Cosy Corner), Queen's Road
This cinema was located a mile west of the town centre. It was opened in 1914 and a little later had a British Thomson Houston sound system installed. From 1950 it was taken over by the Star Cinema chain. Closure came on 24 May 1964 after the showing of *The Thrill of it All*, but the building still survives. Photograph reproduced courtesy of Tony Martin.

Electric Theatre, Commercial Street
In 1910, old stables and a riding school were converted to a cinema becoming the Electric Theatre, operated by National Electric Theatres of London. It opened on 30 July 1910 and seating was for approx. 1,750. Taken over by Denman/Gaumont in 1928, thereafter the building was altered to the plans of Horsefall & Dawson. Further alterations were carried out in 1934 the seating then being for 1,728 patrons. Modernisation carried out in 1939 to the plans of W. E. Trent created a new façade and the seating capacity was noted as being reduced to 1,536. CinemaScope was never installed. Closure came in September 1956 and afterwards the building found use as a car showroom, snooker club and later, following further alterations, a bowling alley and snooker club. Photograph from the Tony Moss Collection and reproduced courtesy of The Cinema Theatre Association.

Electric Theatre, Exley

Halifax Zoo at Exley had an Electric Theatre from *c.* 1912-16, which showed panoramic views. Photograph from the Tony Moss Collection and reproduced courtesy of The Cinema Theatre Association.

Gaiety/Grand Theatre, North Bridge

The Gaiety Theatre was destroyed by fire in 1888 and another building, the Grand Theatre, controlled by Halifax New Grand Theatre & Opera House Co. Ltd, erected on the site. It was designed by Frank Matcham and opened on the 5 August 1889 with a production of *Claudian* by Wilson Barrett and his Company. The proscenium was 28 feet wide, with seating accommodation for 1,650 in stalls, dress circle and upper circle, with two stage boxes and six private boxes. By 1896, it was controlled by the Northern Theatre Co. Ltd. and for the first quarter of the twentieth century there was a mix of films and variety on the entertainment programme. From 1 June 1925, the building was converted for use as a cinema, becoming known as the Grand Picture House and opening with *The Lady Secretary*. In time a Western Electric sound system was added. Later controllers included Charles Denville. Although reverting back to a theatre for a time, and used by the Halifax Theatre Repertory Company, closure came through structural problems in 1956. The Grand was demolished *c.* 1957.

Odeon, Broad Street

The Odeon was designed by eminent architect George Coles and opened on Monday 27 June 1938. The cost of construction amounted to £59,727. There was a small stage and seating was for 2,058: 1,344 stalls and 714 balcony. Closure came on 18 October 1975 after the showing of *Confessions of a Pop Performer*. Both pictures are from the Tony Moss Collection and reproduced courtesy of The Cinema Theatre Association.

Odeon, Broad Street
The Odeon was eventually converted to a Top Rank Club for bingo and later renamed Mecca. The top picture is from the Tony Moss Collection and reproduced courtesy of The Cinema Theatre Association. The one below is a copyright photograph reproduced courtesy of Andrew Riley.

Palace Theatre, Wards End and Southgate

The foundation stone was laid on 4 October 1902. The theatre cost £40,000 to build and was designed by architects Runtz & Co. for Frank MacNaughten. The first performance was on 3 August 1903. Top of the bill was Julie MacKay, the American comedienne. There was seating for 2,500. The proscenium was 30 feet wide and the stage 33 feet deep. Early on, films were shown as part of the variety programme. According to the *Halifax Courier* of Thursday 5 February 2009 the last performance at the Palace was on Saturday, 31 May 1959. It featured Rodgers and Hammerstein's musical *The King And I*, a joint production by Halifax Amateur Operatic and Halifax Light Opera Societies. 'In its five decades, many stars trod its boards, including in 1906, a young Charlie Chaplin,' said the newspaper. A little later, the building was demolished and the site redeveloped. Photograph from the Tony Moss Collection and reproduced courtesy of The Cinema Theatre Association.

Palladium Cinema, King Cross Road

Designed by local architect, Kershaw, the Palladium Picture House opened on 30 March 1914. Seating was for 700 patrons. Subsequent owners included Star Cinemas who took control c. 1945. After undergoing refurbishment the premises were styled New Palladium. Closure came on 18 April 1962 after the showing of *Come September*. Later, the building was converted to a bingo hall and then a carpet warehouse. Photograph from the Tony Moss Collection and reproduced courtesy of The Cinema Theatre Association.

Picturedrome (also known as The Kingston, Kingston Picturedrome & The Lyric) Queen's Road
Erected in 1894 as the Kingston Liberal Club, films were shown there by Albert Greene from 1912. The building held the name Picturedrome for a short time and was also known as the Kingston, Kingston Picturedrome. Under the control of E. B. Ward it became the Lyric. Closure came in July 1951, the venture being described as unviable, but the building is still standing as a bathroom centre. Copyright photograph reproduced courtesy of Tony Martin.

Pioneer (also known as The Ritz and popularly called The Knocker)
This was a small out of town cinema at Wheatley Lane, Ovenden, where Halifax developed its first council housing in the 1930s. On the 1905 O.S. map the building shows as a 'club' but on the 1930 version it is clearly marked as a 'picture house'. Later, the Pioneer (or the Ritz) became part of the Star Cinema chain and closed in February 1963 after a fire. Photograph taken on 25 February 1963 and reproduced courtesy of Tony Martin.

Picture House, Wards End

Designed, according to Hornsey (1995), by Messrs Naylor & Sale and built for Provincial Cinematograph Theatres, the Picture House opened on 2 October 1913. It included cafés, tearooms, a smoking lounge, writing rooms, a large balcony and seating for 1,300.

Picture House, Wards End

Following a fire in 1947 the cinema closed for almost a year, re-opening as the Gaumont. Controllers after PCT included the Gaumont British Picture Corporation Ltd and the Circuits Management Association. A further closure occurred in 1960 and in time the premises were used as a Top Rank Bingo Club (later Surewin). Under lease to Hutchinsons Leisure Ltd from 1973, the old stalls were used for bingo and the old circle divided into two, with 200 seats in each, becoming the Astra Cinema. Both closed on 29 May 1982 but re-opened for a period in June 1983. Then, the premises found use as a nightclub, under the title of the Coliseum, and later as Liquid. The top picture shows the Balcony Promenade at the Picture House, the one below, the Entrance Hall. Both pictures are from the Tony Moss Collection and reproduced courtesy of The Cinema Theatre Association.

Picture House, Wards End
The building gained Grade II listing status on 5 October 2000 and on www.britishlistedbuildings.
co.uk it is said: 'The principal and right-hand façades of the cinema are rich examples of the
Edwardian Baroque style.' Both pictures are from the Tony Moss Collection and reproduced
courtesy of The Cinema Theatre Association.

Playhouse Theatre, King Cross Street
Halifax Thespians formed in October 1927 and their first play *Dear Brutus* was performed as a matinée at the Theatre Royal during March 1928. Then, in 1931 the group moved to the Alexandra Hall but fourteen years later they purchased the Hanover Methodist Church for £2,500. The conversion work was carried out to the designs of local architects Arthur Pickles and Cyril Sunderland. The proscenium arch is 26 feet wide and the stage 18 feet deep. The seating capacity is 260. The first production *The Merry Wives of Windsor* was performed at the Playhouse Theatre in September 1949. Photograph reproduced courtesy of Halifax Playhouse Theatre.

Theatre Cinema-de-Luxe/Roxy-de-Luxe, Northgate
The cinema opened on 11 March 1912 in the old Northgate Hall. The premises accommodated approx. 500 patrons and in 1934 after being sold to Messrs J. & H. Buxton became known as the Roxy-de-Luxe. The cinema operated until December 1938. Photograph from the Tony Moss Collection and reproduced courtesy of The Cinema Theatre Association.

Regal/ABC, Ward's End

Designed by architect William R. Glen, for the Associated British Cinemas, the Regal Cinema opened on 19 September 1938. There were 1,940 seats for patrons. The proscenium arch was 55 feet wide, the stage 12 feet deep and there were four dressing rooms. Hornsey (1995) states that no organ was installed until 1941. The building was renamed ABC in 1961 (with 1,173 seats for customers) and provided three screens from September 1976. It was renamed Canon c. 1986 and then reverted back to ABC before closure in 2002. Grade II listing status had been awarded by English Heritage on 5 October 2000. On www.imagesofengland.org.uk it is stated: 'Virtually all the cinemas built by Associated British Cinemas in the 1930s have now been drastically altered or demolished, making [the Halifax] one, with much surviving original decoration, a rarity.' The photograph below is from the Tony Moss Collection and reproduced courtesy of The Cinema Theatre Association.

Theatre Royal and Opera House, Ward's End, Southgate

An earlier Theatre Royal existed on the site between 1789 and 1904. Former controllers of the theatre were a Mr Pero, and Messrs Taylor & Robertson. The last performance staged there was *Old Kentucky*, on 5 March 1904. The new Theatre Royal, designed by Richard Horsfall & Son of Halifax, was opened by the Mayor of Halifax Ald. Enoch Robinson on Friday, 4 August, 1905. The event also marked the first public performance, at the theatre, given by the Halifax Amateur Operatic Society, who staged *The Mikado*. Seating was for approx. 2,000 people. The first professional performance – a comedy, *Our Flat* – was given on 14 August 1904. On www. theatrestrust.org.uk it is said that the premises were altered after a fire in 1927. Hornsey (1995) states that a fire during 1937 ended its days as a theatre, adding: '[I]t spurred on the owners, Northern Theatres Limited to refurbish and convert it into a more 1930s style of cinema.' Top photograph from the Tony Moss Collection and reproduced courtesy of The Cinema Theatre Association.

Theatre Royal and Opera House, Ward's End, Southgate
Matthew Lloyd on www.arthurlloyd.co.uk says the building was converted to a Bingo Hall in 1966 and closed in 1992. Thereafter the building, which gained Grade II listing status in May 1994 was used as entertainment café called La Manía, and a nightclub – Club Platinum. The photograph was taken on 23 February 1966.

Victoria/Theatre, Fountain Street

The Victoria Hall was designed by architect W. Clement Williams for the Halifax Concert Hall & Public Rooms Co. Ltd and opened on 8 February 1901 with a concert by the Halle Orchestra. In 1960 the hall was purchased by Halifax Borough Council who undertook an extensive alteration and repair programme 1962-66 and converted it into a theatre and changed the name to The New Victoria. In 1973 the name was changed to The Civic Theatre, before being renamed The Victoria Theatre in 1993. The Theatre's website states: 'Boasting an impressive main auditorium with a capacity of 1,512 fully-seated (and 1,860 part-standing), the theatre plays host to many high profile and international performers and artistes as well as serving and supporting a wide range of the local community events and activities.' The Victoria Theatre was given Grade II listing status by English Heritage on 24 June 1997. The picture below was taken on 8 January 1960.

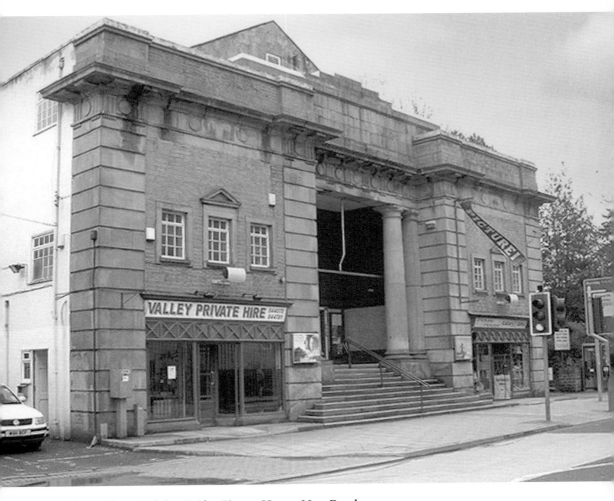

Hebden Bridge – Hebden Bridge Picture House, New Road

Hebden Bridge Picture House opened in 1921. Originally boasting over 900 seats its first screening was a double bill of *Torn Sails* and *The Iron Stair*. The cinema's website states that in the late 1960s, when many of the mills had closed, the Picture House nearly suffered the fate of so many town cinemas and was very close to becoming a carpet warehouse. It was saved for the town by the actions of the then Hebden Royd Urban District Council who purchased the Picture House from its private owners for the sum of about £6,000. The cinema passed into Calderdale Councils control with local government reorganisation in 1973, and CMBC oversaw a subsequent refurbishment in 1978, removing half of the seats and leaving the current 492 seats with their often praised generous legroom. The website adds that in 1999, the future of the Picture House again appeared to be at risk when the site was earmarked for development. A strong community campaign, Friends of the Picture House, rapidly mobilised and following a mass lobby of the Calderdale MBC full council in July 1999 the development plans were rejected, and the future of the Picture House secured. As one campaigner put it at the time, "I speak of 'Our' Picture House ... it has become part of our heritage." Since then the Picture House has blossomed, as one of the very few cinemas in Britain under municipal ownership.' During 2012 Picture House was transferred back to Hebden Royd Town Council (the body that replaced Hebden Royd Urban District Council) who originally took the Picture House into civic ownership in the late 1960s. Copyright photograph reproduced courtesy of Nigel Homer.

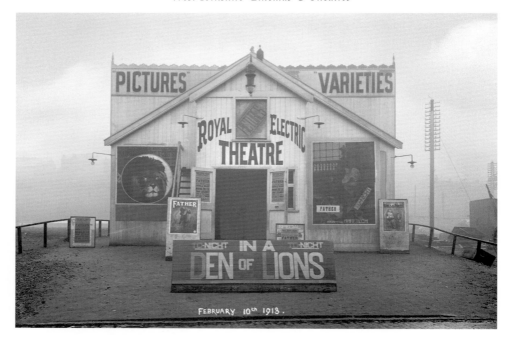

Hebden Bridge Royal Electric Theatre
The Royal Electric Theatre is pictured on 10 February 1913. Photograph reproduced courtesy of the Pennine Horizons Digital Archive.

Sowerby Bridge – Electric Theatre/Roxy, Wharf Street
The Electric Theatre opened on 25 November 1915 with seating for 812 patrons. Later controllers included Gaumont British Theatres and Star Cinemas. In time it was re-named Roxy and closed in February 1963. The building subsequently found use as a bingo hall and café, and a nightclub and bar. Copyright photograph reproduced courtesy of Andrew Riley.

Regent/Essoldo, Wharf Street

The Regent opened on 28 December 1939. Seating was for approx. 914. It was renamed Essoldo when taken over by Essoldo Cinemas chain in March 1949. Closure came on 4 February 1967 after the showing of Elvis Presley in *GI Blues* and Jerry Lewis in *The Caddy*. Later the building was used as a nightclub and an indoor market. Demolition occurred in 1987 though the frontage was retained. The photograph dates from 2 February 1967.

Todmorden – Hippodrome, Halifax Road

Todmorden's Hippodrome opened as a live theatre on 5 October 1908 with Hardie and Von Leer's Company in *Two Lancashire Lasses in London*. On www.todhip.org it is stated: 'It was the brainchild of Richard Dewhirst, who took land abutting his shop and printing works in Halifax Road on which to build his theatre. An ambitious project which, although it was scaled down from the original design of stalls, circle and gallery, could still seat 1000 when it opened...' But, Richard Dewhirst was bankrupt by 1911. The theatre was sold and, in September 1912, passed to the Hartleys who had theatre and cinema interests in Nelson and Burnley. The website adds: '[They] were always sympathetic to local societies, who had used the stage for musicals and plays as early as 1909.' The Hartleys closed the Hippodrome during 1956 and it was leased by the Todmorden Operatic Society who, along with the Todmorden Players, continued to perform there. In 1986 Todmorden Amateur Operatic and Dramatic Society came into being when the two groups merged. When the Hartleys decided to sell the Hippodrome in 1987 they gave first refusal to TAODS, who acquired the theatre for £28,000. Seating presently is for 495 patrons. Copyright photograph reproduced courtesy of Betty Longbottom.

Todmorden – New Olympia, Burnley Road

A roller skating rink opened on this site in 1909 but was converted to the Olympia cinema a year later. Existing until May 1931, it was replaced by the New Olympia Cinema which was designed in the Art Deco style by Burnley-based architectural firm of Aspen & Johnson and opened on 25 August 1932. Later owners included the Star Cinema chain but it closed as a cinema in 1966 to become a Star Bingo Club. Later, the building became a bingo hall and then a Kwik Save supermarket. The latter closed in around 2008. The top picture is reproduced courtesy of Roger Birch, the one below Andrew Riley.

Kirklees

Batley – Regent/Regency Bradford Road

The Regent operated from *c*. 1919 to *c*. 1963. At one time it offered over 800 seats for patrons. Thereafter the building was used for bingo, showing Asian films, and latterly accommodated the Regency restaurant. The picture dates from July 1979. The *Yorkshire Evening Post* of 10 July 1979 stated: 'The clock will go back 16 years later this month when the old Regent Cinema re-opens to fill another gap in Batley's sparse entertainment programme. The enterprise which give[s] Batley back a cinema once more, is being undertaken by a Bradford family. Mr Manzoor Ahmed Bhatti and his two sons of Bertram Road, will achieve one of their long-held ambitions of becoming cinema proprietors. The cinema will be called The Regency, but it will still be the Regent to thousands of local folks who have their own special memories of the building.'

Birstall – Princess Picture House, Market Street
The cinema was built in 1919 along with the surrounding shops. Later it became part of the Star Cinema chain. It is now partly used as a dance studio. The building was photographed on 2 January 2006 by Humphrey Bolton.

Showcase Cinema, Gelderd Road
Showcase Cinemas opened on 14 December 1989 with 12 screens, increased to 14 in 1997 and 16 two years later. The seating accommodation is for approx. 4,000. The cinema is pictured under construction on 11 November 1989.

The Showcase Cinema pictured on 23 October 1997.

Cleckheaton – Picture Palace, Albion Street
Local businessman Walter Goodall built the Picture Palace in 1911. Later it became part of the
Star Cinema chain. It closed after a fire in 1960.

Savoy, Bradford Road
The Savoy was built by Walter Goodall and opened in 1923. Later it became part of the Star Cinema chain. The building was demolished in 1990 and the site was derelict for a number of years but was landscaped in 2003.

Dewsbury – Empire Theatre, Wakefield Road
Designed by architects Chadwick & Watson, the Empire Theatre opened with a variety show on 2 August 1909. The opening ceremony was attended by the Mayor of Dewsbury, Ald F. W. Reuss. Seating, for approx. 2,000, was on three levels: stalls and two circles. The stage was 30 feet deep and the building boasted eight dressing rooms. Films were shown on occasions and a Western Electric sound system was installed in 1934. The Empire was especially noted for its annual Christmas pantomimes often stretching from Christmas Eve until the middle of March each year.

Empire Theatre, Wakefield Road
A performance by the Dewsbury Operatic Society was the last stage show at the Empire in April 1955 and it was demolished around five years later. Empire House – an office block – was eventually built on the site.

Hippodrome/Picturehouse, Foundry Street
The original Hippodrome was built in 1880 but destroyed by fire in 1896. The premises were rebuilt in the same year and demolished in 1950.

Picture House, Market Place
The Picture House opened its doors on 12 July 1913. The building was converted to a twin screen cinema on 31 June 1969 with 330 seats in the former stalls and 144 in the circle. Over the years it underwent several name changes: Regal Super Cinema, December 1933; Essoldo, *c.* 1955; Classic Cinema, 1972; Cannon, *c.* 1975; Apollo Cinema, *c.* 1992. Latterley, it was used as a Homeland bedding shop, but the auditorium was demolished in April 2009. The slim entrance is still extant. The picture on the right dates from October 1958.

Picture House, Market Place
The remaining frontage of the cinema
photographed on 28 April 1993.

Playhouse Theatre, Crackenedge Lane
The Playhouse Theatre was designed Robert Cromie for Lou Morris. It opened on 26 October
1931 and was used for theatre and cinema. Seating – on two levels: stalls and one circle – was for
1,850 people. The proscenium was 50 feet wide; there were six dressing rooms and a Compton
3Manual/8Ranks organ was installed. The premises became part of the Associated British
Cinemas(ABC) chain from 6 May 1935 though not re-named ABC until 1963. Pop concerts were
also held there. Closure as a cinema came on 11 December 1970. Thereafter the building was used
for bingo but eventually demolished in 2002. A Wilkinson's Store currently occupies the site.

Heckmondwike – Pavilion
The Pavilion opened in January 1914 with films and variety turns and closed in December 1962.

Holmfirth – Holme Valley Theatre/Picturedrome, Market Street
The Picturedrome was built in 1912 and was originally known as the Holme Valley Theatre. Opening on Easter Monday, 1 March 1913 it seated 1,040 people – 240 in the balcony and 800 downstairs. The Picturedrome's website states that the first films to be shown in the Valley Theatre were: *A Court Intrigue*, *That Awful Pipe* and *Betrayed by a Kiss*. 'In the first 10 to 15 years, the theatre presented its audience with a large variety of live acts including musicians, actors and even a stage appearance of a strong man billed as Yorkshire's Hercules. The first sound feature was the popular 'Sunnyside Up', which opened on 13 October 1930. The same year, the auditorium had been re-decorated and re-carpeted, and a new screen was installed with electrically operated curtains, while dimmers had been fitted to the lights. The projection system was greatly improved as was the sound system,' states the website. Over the years the seating capacity was gradually reduced and by 1952 the building could accommodate 779 customers. It is pictured here after a flood caused by cloudburst on Whit Monday 29 May 1944.

Holme Valley Theatre/Picturedrome, Market Street

With dwindling audiences, The Valley Theatre closed on Saturday 16 September 1967 with *The Family Way* starring John Mills. Still owned by the Valley Picture Theatre Company, it was leased to Bradford Amusement Caterers and reopened as a bingo hall on Wednesday, 20 December 1967. Bingo continued for some 26 years but then the theatre was unused. Plans to reopen it as a cinema came to nothing. Towards the end of 1997 it was purchased by Andrew Bottomley and eventually leased to Peter and Rachel Carr in November 1998, who later bought the building in 2003. The ground floor was utilised as a cinema capable of staging live performances. The cinema, becoming known as the Picturedrome, closed in 2007, but following public protests, re-opened in January 2008. From 2009 programming has been largely live music, though films are still shown, and the stage is used for occasional theatre performances. Copyright photograph reproduced courtesy of Kenny Allen.

Huddersfield – Empire Cinema, John William Street

Local architects Stocks & Sykes were responsible for the design of the Empire Cinema for the proprietors Huddersfield Entertainments Ltd and it opened on 8 March 1915. The stalls and a single balcony provided seating for 800. *Kismet* was the first film shown. During the early 1920s the cinema was controlled by Lion Picture House and Estate (Huddersfield) Ltd and then came under Max Goldstone. The first full-length talkie film was screened on 21 October 1929, the *Trial of Mary Duggan*. From the early 1930s the premises were leased to Associated British Cinemas (ABC) and extensive renovations were carried out in 1940. It re-opened as the New Empire and was leased to the J. F. Emery circuit. Further improvements to the building were undertaken April 1951 and April 1952 during which time the cinema was closed. In the same decade Goldstones sold the building to Messrs Ryans. Closure came on Saturday 4 August 1973. Eventually, there was a concentration on adult films and internally the building has under gone much alteration, being divided for other commercial purposes whilst still showing films on a much reduced scale. On 29 September 1978, it gained Grade II listing status from English Heritage.

Excelda, Lockwood
Designed by J. Berry & Son the cinema was opened by the Excelda Picture Palace Co. on 18 November 1915. Mrs Mary Blamire, Mayoress of Huddersfied, attended the opening ceremony. The first film shown was *Jane Eyre*. Seating was for 1,080 and Western Electric Sound was added in 1930. After closure *c.* 1960 the premises found use as a factory by the Rolla Sheet Metal Co. Ltd. Photograph from the Tony Moss Collection and reproduced courtesy of The Cinema Theatre Association.

Grand Picture Theatre, Manchester Road
Architect Clifford Hickson of Huddersfield firm Stocks & Sykes designed the cinema which opened on 14 March 1921 at a cost of £32,000. The Mayoress of Huddersfield Miss Wolven officiated at the opening ceremony. The building provided accommodation for 687 and the proscenium was 28 feet wide. The opening film was *J'accuse*. Photograph from the Tony Moss Collection and reproduced courtesy of The Cinema Theatre Association.

Grand Picture Theatre, Manchester Road

'Talkies' were introduced at the Grand from 10 June 1929 when a Western Electric sound system was added. Operators of the cinema included Union Cinemas (from 1929) and (under a management agreement) Associated British Cinemas (from November 1937). Closure came on 6 June 1957 after the showing of *The Man from Colorado* and *Hour of Decision*. For time the building staged jazz and rock concerts and operated as a nightclub under the name Eros then Ivanhoe. The latter closed 1992/93 and the interior was eventually demolished and redeveloped. The French Renaissance/Greek Revival-style façade survives. Both photographs are from the Tony Moss Collection and reproduced courtesy of The Cinema Theatre Association.

Hippodrome (formerly The Armoury Theatre)/Essoldo/Classic/Cannon/Tudor, Queensgate
A building erected as riding shed, during February 1848, found use as a theatre (The Armoury) and drill hall during the remaining years of the century. Animated pictures were also shown there in 1900. Two years later the Northern Theatre Company acquired the building and it became The Armoury Theatre. By July 1905 the company had converted it to a music hall, styled the Hippodrome, and seats were provided for 1,500 patrons.

Hippodrome (formerly The Armoury Theatre)/Essoldo/Classic/Cannon/Tudor, Queensgate
Films were shown as part of the entertainment up to 1930 when, after refurbishment, the building opened as the Tudor House Super Cinema. The 'talkies' arrived there in October 1933 with the screening of *Cavalcade*. During the 1950s the cinema became part of the Essoldo Circuit and was renamed Essoldo from Monday 18 November 1957. A blaze severely damaged the cinema in December 1967 but it was rebuilt, and opened with seats for a mere 495. Later, in the 1970s, the building was taken over by the Classic Cinema Circuit, and became the Classic and in turn, Cannon when it passed to the Cannon Circuit. Both photographs are from the Tony Moss Collection and reproduced courtesy of The Cinema Theatre Association.

Hippodrome (formerly The Armoury Theatre)/Essoldo/Classic/Cannon/Tudor, Queensgate
A fire in May 1992 caused further damage to the building and in 1995 it was leased to Page Media Holdings who renamed it Tudor. But in time, it became a bar, called Livingstones until 2010. Copyright photograph reproduced courtesy of Humphrey Bolton.

Lounge, Newsome Road
Designed by architect Joe Ainley, the cinema was opened by the Lounge Cinema Co. on 15 December 1937. The first film was *Maytime*. The proscenium was 30 feet wide and there was seating for 720 patrons. The premises closed *c.* 1960 and the last film screened was *Operation Petticoat*. Photograph from the Tony Moss Collection and reproduced courtesy of The Cinema Theatre Association.

Lyceum, Wakefield Road

The Lyceum Cinema (Moldgreen) Ltd opened the Lyceum at 2.30 p.m. on 6 February 1922 with seating for 988 (733 in the stalls and 255 in the circle). The proscenium was 26 feet wide and the first film shown was *Peck's Bad Boy*. A BTH Sound system was added in 1930 and the building suffered fire damage on 23 March 1934. Subsequent controllers included Moldgreen Entertainment Ltd, the Star Cinema chain, J. F. Emery and C. E. Mison. The cinema closed c. 1959. Photograph from the Tony Moss Collection and reproduced courtesy of The Cinema Theatre Association.

Palace Theatre, Kirkgate

Designed by Horsfall & Sons, the Palace opened in 1909 with seating for 1,164. The stage was 60 feet wide and 30 feet deep. The initial controllers were the McNaghten Vaudeville Circuit. Films were shown occasionally during the theatre's early years. After being gutted by fire in January 1936, the premises were rebuilt in an Art Deco style to the design of architects Roland Satchwell and Ernest S. Roberts and is one of only two remaining examples of the pair's work. Between 1963 and 1997 the building was used for bingo. Then, it became a Chicago Rock Café and later a nightclub under the titles, Shout and Society. Photograph from the Tony Moss Collection and reproduced courtesy of The Cinema Theatre Association.

Palladium, Blacker Road, Birkby

J. Hall & Sons of Huddersfield designed and built the Palladium cinema for the proprietors the Palladium Picture Company (Birkby) Ltd. It opened on 16 March 1913. Seating was for around 500 persons and sound was installed in December 1930. The cinema closed on 20 February 1937 and was partly demolished and rebuilt, opening on 30 August 1937, becoming known as the Carlton. Seating was for 674 and the proscenium was 22 feet in width. The man behind the venture was J. H. Freer and the new proprietors were Regal Cinema Co. Moldgreen Ltd. The opening ceremony was attended by the Mayor elect of Huddersfield Alderman A. Willis. The first films screened were *Good Morning Boys* and *Sabotage*. From 1942 the cinema was controlled by F. & H. Cinemas Ltd. In *Ninety Years of Cinema in Huddersfield* (1998) Brian Hornsey states the Palladium closed around 10 July 1954 after the showing of *The Intruder* and *Beneath the Seven Seas*. Then, the premises were converted for use as a bingo hall and later as a mosque. The photograph below is from the Tony Moss Collection and reproduced courtesy of The Cinema Theatre Association.

Picturedrome/Curzon, Buxton Road

Architects, Schofield & Sons, designed the Picturedrome for proprietors Hibbert's Pictures and it opened on 2 December 1910. The first films shown included *A Tragedy in Toyland* and the opening ceremony was attended by the Mayor of Huddersfield. During 1913 the premises were altered and the seating then provided for 890 patrons. Sound was introduced to the Picturedrome in April 1929. In the following decade variety shows were occasionally staged and a fire closed the building for a time in September 1949. Later controllers of the cinema included Walker & Newton Cinemas Ltd. Closure came on 27 August 1950 after the showing of *Bush Pilot* and *King of the Stallions*. Photograph from the Tony Moss Collection and reproduced courtesy of The Cinema Theatre Association.

Picture House/Essoldo, Ramsden Street

Designed by A. C. Haigh, and with seating for 600 (later increased to 873), the Picture House was opened by proprietors, the Northern Theatre Company of Halifax, on 26 December 1912. There were 600 seats for patrons, but a balcony added in 1920 seated a further 125. The cinema was situated adjacent to the Theatre Royal and the first films shown were *The Incredible Stain* and *The Red Ink Tragedy*. Sound was installed during November 1930. Later controllers included the Essoldo Cinemas chain and closure came in June 1967. The last films shown were *The Quartermass Experiment* and *X the Unknown*. Thereafter the building was demolished. Photograph from the Tony Moss Collection and reproduced courtesy of The Cinema Theatre Association.

Picture House/Essoldo, Ramsden Street
Interior view of the Picture House/Essoldo. Photograph from the Tony Moss Collection and reproduced courtesy of The Cinema Theatre Association.

Princess Picture House, Northumberland Street
On Saturday 19 May 1923, the Princess Picture House opened in a building that was formerly a wool merchant's warehouse (once occupied by Herbert Dickinson & Sons). Designs for the conversion work were carried out by Huddersfield architect Capt. Clifford Hickson of Stott, Sykes & Hickson. Film star Miss Peggy Hyland attended the opening ceremony. The first film shown to an invited audience was *Shifting Sands*, and the first shown to the general public was *Way Down East*. Seating was for 900 patrons. Costing around £34,000, the building also incorporated a café in the basement (opening on 19 October 1923). The proscenium was 26 feet wide and operators of the cinema included Princess Picture Palace Ltd. CinemaScope was added by 1959.

Princess Picture House, Northumberland Street
The building gained Grade II listing status from English Heritage on 29 September 1978. Richard Gere in *Yanks* was the last film shown on 24 April 1982. In subsequent years the building has found use as a restaurant, nightclub and casino. Photograph from the Tony Moss Collection and reproduced courtesy of The Cinema Theatre Association.

Regal, Wakefield Road, Moldgreen
Opening on 6 April 1936, the first film screened was *The Guvnor*. Hornsey (1998) notes that 'the front part of the building was a private residence.' Seating was for approx. 820. Later controllers included the Star Cinema chain. From the 1960s bingo was part of the entertainment programme for two nights of the week initially. The last films were shown in September 1962 though bingo continued for a short time afterwards. The building was razed to the ground in February 1988. Photograph from the Tony Moss Collection and reproduced courtesy of The Cinema Theatre Association.

Regent Cinema, Bradford Road, Fartown
A showing of the film *Cavalcade* opened the Regent on 11 November 1933. It was designed in the Art Deco style by local architect J. H. Freer for the Regent Cinema Company (Fartown) Limited. Seating was for approx. 668 and a B.T.H sound system was included. Fire severely damaged the building on 16 June 1936 and the renovation work took until September of that year to be completed. Later operators included the Star Cinema chain, Regent (Huddersfield) Ltd and F. & H. Cinemas. From the 1960s, the building was used as a bingo hall, a dance hall, the Regent night club (later Vanity Fair), a fun pub, and restaurant. It suffered fire damage in 1983 and following renovation became an Indian restaurant. Photograph from the Tony Moss Collection and reproduced courtesy of The Cinema Theatre Association.

Rialto Cinema, Brackenhall Road, Sheepbridge
Designed by J. H. Freer, the cinema opened (according to Tony Moss's notes held by the CTA) on 3 November 1938. A formal opening was attended by Councillor and Mrs James R Gregson, along with Joan Ellum who featured in the opening film *South Riding*. The venue provided seating for approx. 820 and the proscenium opening was 26 feet wide. Controllers included F. & H. Cinemas; CinemaScope was fitted in later years. Following closure c. 1960 the building was converted into a Catholic Church. Photograph from the Tony Moss Collection and reproduced courtesy of The Cinema Theatre Association.

Ritz/ABC, Market Street

Built to the designs of Richard Cromie by the Union Cinemas chain, the Ritz Cinema opened on 10 February 1936. It had cost around £100,000 to complete and included a proscenium approx. 50 feet wide, and a 28 feet deep stage with seven dressing rooms. There was also £10,000 Wurlitzer organ. The opening ceremony was attended by Councillor J. Barlow, Mayor of Huddersfield. The first film shown was Jessie Mathews in *First A Girl*. Seating in the stalls and circle was for 2,036 people and adjacent at circle level was a café. Both photographs are from the Tony Moss Collection and reproduced courtesy of The Cinema Theatre Association.

Ritz/ABC, Market Street

Associated British Cinemas (ABC) took control in October 1937 and improvements in the 1950s included the installation of a new screen in September 1953 and CinemaScope shortly afterwards. A change of name to ABC occurred in 1961. In the following years, the cinema underwent various alterations, including establishing a pub in one area, and having split screens and live performances in others. The ABC closed on 5 March 1983 and was demolished in June 1985. Photograph from the Tony Moss Collection and reproduced courtesy of The Cinema Theatre Association.

Savoy, Westbourne Road, Marsh

The Savoy Picture House (Huddersfield) Ltd opened the cinema on Thursday 19 February 1920. The first film screened was *A Tale of Two Cities* and there were approx. 900 seats for patrons. 'Talkies' arrived at the Savoy in October 1926. Subsequent controllers included Mark Friedman and Walker & Newton Cinemas Ltd. Renovations took place in 1947 and in the following decade CinemaScope was added. From the early 1960s bingo became part of the week's entertainment programme and in time the building was converted to a supermarket. Photograph from the Tony Moss Collection and reproduced courtesy of The Cinema Theatre Association.

Savoy, Skelmanthorpe

The cinema was built *c*. 1934 and existed solely as such until 1961 when wrestling was introduced to increase receipts. Closure as a cinema occurred *c*. 1968 and thereafter the building has found use as a bingo hall, a squash club and Youth Centre. Copyright photograph reproduced courtesy of Barry Watchorn.

Theatre Royal, Ramsden Street/Bull and Mouth Street

The original Theatre Royal (built as a Lecture Hall by the Philosophical Society) existed from the early 1840s until 1859. It was re-modelled by builder John Yondon to the designs of a Mr Cocking and opened on 24 of September of the latter year. The new theatre followed several changes of directions under different lessees (including Herr Teasdale, W. S. Thorne and John Hudspeth) until 1880 when building was destroyed by fire. Rebuilding took place to the designs of B. E. Entwistle for J. A. Love and the new theatre opened on 11 April 1881 with a production of *As You Like It*. The stage was 55 foot wide with a proscenium opening of 26 feet by 28 feet. The Gallery and Pit could each accommodate around 1,000 patrons; the Dress Circle approx. 120 and the Upper Circle approx. 130. The building was demolished in February 1961 by Huddersfield Corporation. The final production was *Sailor Beware*. The photograph dates from 1 March 1961.

Victoria Temperance Hall/Victoria Hall/New Victoria Hall Theatre

The Victoria Temperance Hall was opened by the Huddersfield Temperance Society on 1 March 1879. It showed films from around May 1898 and was known as the Victoria Hall from October 1900. It became a permanent cinema during September 1914 and seating was for between 600 and 700 patrons. Closure as a regular film venue came on 14 February 1931 after the showing of *The Concentratin' Kid*. From February 1933 the building operated as the New Victoria Theatre and produced live stage shows, closure coming again in March 1938. Former controllers included Henry Kaye. Photograph from the Tony Moss Collection and reproduced courtesy of The Cinema Theatre Association.

Waterloo Cinema, Wakefield Road, Waterloo

Opening on Monday 12 October 1931, the Waterloo Cinema had seating for around 1,000. Designed by Halifax architect, C. E. Mallinson, the building also featured a stage and dressing rooms. *Beau Ideal* was the first film show. Amongst the controllers were Waterloo Cinema Company and the Star Cinema chain. CinemaScope was added in the mid-1950s and bingo featured during a period in the 1960s before the building was converted to a supermarket, Lodges.

Leeds City Centre

ABC (formerly Ritz Cinema), Vicar Lane, Leeds
Proprietors Associated Cinemas Ltd, employed in-house architect W. R. Glen to produce plans for the Ritz which opened on Monday 19 November 1934. *Those Were the Days* was the first film shown and seating was available for 1,100 in the stalls and 850 in the circle. From 23 May 1959, the name was changed to ABC. The photograph dates from 2 April 1970.

ABC (formerly Ritz Cinema), Vicar Lane, Leeds

Conversion of the ABC to a twin cinema occurred on 5 April 1970 with 620 seats in the former stalls and 867 in the former circle, when the opening films were *Paint Your Wagon* and *Spring and Port Wine*. Then, on Sunday 17 March 1974 ABC 2 was divided into two screens with 474 and 236 seats and the building became Leed's first triple cinema, screening *The Sting*, *Paper Moon* and *Walking Tall*. Both photographs date from 2 April 1970.

Above left: **Cannon (formerly Ritz Cinema and ABC), Vicar Lane, Leeds**
The ABC became the Cannon in March 1987, then the MGM in 1991 but reverted back to ABC in 1993. Closure came in February 2000 with screen 1 showing *American Beauty*, screen 2 *Double Jeopardy* and the Bollywood film *Shaheed Uddham Singh* in screen 3. The building was demolished in February 2006. The photograph dates from 15 June 1987.

Above right: **City Varieties, Swan Street/The Headrow**
The City Varieties is a surviving example of a Victorian Music Hall and was opened on 7 June 1865 as an extension to the music room of the White Swan Inn. It was designed by George Smith for Charles Thornton who had been landlord at the White Swan since 1857. For a time the premises were known as Thornton's New Music Hall and Fashionable Lounge and then between 1877 and 1884 were listed as the Stansfield Varieties. By the end of the nineteenth century the name City Varieties was adopted and has remained ever since. The picture was taken on 31 December 1968.

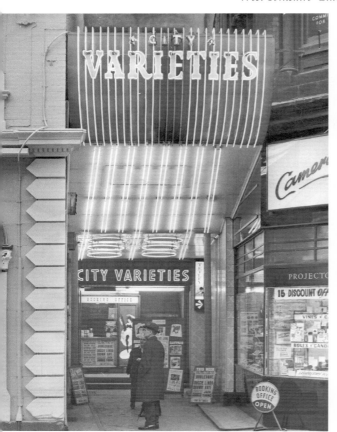 

City Varieties, Swan Street/The Headrow

During its existence the building has undergone many ownership changes and was finally purchased by Leeds City Council in 1988. Between 1953 and 1983, the theatre achieved national fame as the venue for the BBC television programme *The Good Old Days*, a recreation of old-time music hall featuring Leonard Sachs as the alliterative Chairman. On 15 February 1960 the City Varieties achieved Grade II listing status. The theatre closed for refurbishment in January 2009, and re-opened in September 2011. The costs totalled £9.2 million which was partly funded by Leeds City Council (£5.2 million) and the Heritage Lottery Fund (£2.74 million). At the re-opening the physical link between the Swan Inn and the theatre was re-established. Prior to being purchased by Leeds City Council the premises had been with the Joseph family; Stanley and Michael Joseph are pictured here (on the right), 18 August 1987. The photograph on the left was taken on 5 February 1970.

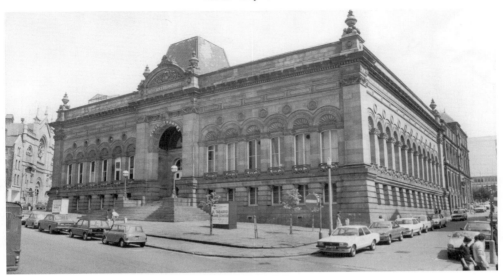

Civic Theatre, Cookridge Street

The building which later housed the Civic Theatre was completed in 1868 to the designs of Cuthbert Brodrick the Leeds architect who had produced plans for the Town Hall, and the Corn Exchange. Opening as the Mechanics' Institute, (or more commonly the Institute of Arts and Science), in the main part of the building was a circular lecture hall called the Albert Hall, and this eventually housed the Civic Theatre. It measured 73 feet in diameter, was 52 feet high and could accommodate 1,500 spectators. From the 1920s onwards the building was used as a theatre and by 1925, was named the Civic Playhouse after being taken over by the British Drama League. Admission was free, but a collection was taken at each performance, and patrons could support the theatre by becoming subscribers. Alterations took place in 1949 and the building was officially opened as the Civic Theatre on 7 October of that year. During 1983 Claire Ferraby was commissioned to re-design the Civic. The work included re-modelling the proscenium, renovating the auditorium, redecorating the ceiling, and restoration of the chandelier. Thereafter the Civic put on a diverse programme of drama, concerts and recitals, light entertainment, opera and operettas, dance, pantomime, and children's shows. The Civic closed in 2005 and the building reopened as the City Museum in 2008. The top picture dates from 30 July 1993, the one below 23 January 1968.

Classic (formerly News Theatre), Queens Hotel Building, City Square
The News Theatre opened at noon on Monday 22 August 1938 with a special opening programme which included *Golf Mistakes*, *Popeye* and *Radio Parade*. Bedford architect Cecil Massey was responsible for the design and there were 290 seats. Several name changes followed: Classic, 4 September 1966, Tatler Film Club, 17 February 1969 and Classic, 15 July 1979.

Coliseum, Cookridge Street
Designed by W. Bakewell, the building initially opened in the presence of the Prince and Princess of Wales (who were visiting Leeds) on Wednesday 15 July 1885 as a concert hall and variety theatre. It seated as many as 3,000. The old panorama shows, forerunners of motion pictures, were frequently put on at the Coliseum. Circus shows, too, were common. It was also hired on occasion by Sydney Carter to show pictures and he opened the Coliseum showing 'New Century Animated Pictures' on Monday 17 April 1905. Amongst the first films shown were *A Holiday in Paris* and *A Visit to the Celebrated Fountains at Versailles*. When he moved to the Assembly Rooms on New Briggate in 1907, the North British Animated Films Co. continued to show pictures there. In 1928 the Theatre was taken over by Denman/Gaumont, and ten years later, after considerable work on the interior, reopened on Monday 24 October 1938 as the Gaumont-Coliseum with seating for 1,700 patrons. The architects responsible for the conversion were W. Sydney Trent & Daniel Mackay. The opening films were *Snow White and the Seven Dwarfs* and *Rhythm on the Ranch* with Gene Autry and Smiley Burnette. Since closure on Saturday 23 December 1961 the building has been used in a number of ways. It was a bingo hall until 1969; utilised by Leeds Playhouse for Theatre in Education; a film and TV studio run by Colosseum until 1991; a nightclub called Creation which closed in 2004 and is currently a venue known as the 02 Academy owned by AMG (Academy Music Group). Photograph reproduced courtesy of Matthew Lloyd.

Empire Palace Theatre

Seating over 1, 700 patrons, the Empire Palace Theatre was designed by Frank Matcham for the Liverpool, Leeds & Hull Empire Palaces Limited. It opened on 29 August 1898 and seventeen acts were featured, amongst them being Lydia Yeamans (the original *Sally in our Alley*), the French comedian O'Gust, Harry Tate impersonating Dan Leno and others, and John Higgins, the Human Kangaroo. The Theatre was altered in 1931 enabling it to show films as well as regular Variety. Cliff Richard appeared there in the late 1950s but in the following decade, the site was redeveloped. Emile Littler's *Babes in the Wood*, starring Nat Jackley, was the last show on 25 February 1961. The building was demolished in 1962, and replaced by the Empire Arcade, presently housing Harvey Nichols department store. The bottom picture shows the Leeds Empire's last audience on 25 February 1961.

Grand Theatre, New Briggate

Built at a cost of £62,000, the Grand opened on 18 November 1878 with a performance of William Shakespeare's *Much Ado About Nothing*. It was designed by George Corson (1829–1910), a Scottish architect active in Leeds, along with his assistant James Robinson Watson. The exterior design reflects a mixture of Romanesque and Scottish baronial styles, while the interior features Gothic motifs: fan-vaulting and clustered columns. It achieved Grade II listing status on 15 February 1960. The picture below was taken on 1 September 1982.

Grand Theatre, New Briggate

A major refurbishment was started at the Grand Theatre in 2005 resulting in the closure of the theatre until October 2006 when it reopened with a production of Verdi's *Rigoletto*. The refurbishment had included re-seating and re-raking the stalls, the enlargement of the orchestra-pit, installing air conditioning, and improving the backstage areas. Also, Opera North now has an Opera Centre to the south of the theatre, accessible via a bridge and at street-level. The Centre includes two new stage-sized rehearsal spaces and increased office space. The cost of the refurbishment has been estimated at around £31.5 million. A second phase of refurbishment included structural improvements and further refurbishment of the theatre, and also the restoration of the adjacent Assembly Rooms. The Grand is regularly visited by Northern Ballet and at the present time provides 1,500 seats for patrons. The picture shows the theatre from the stage.

Leeds Playhouse

Leeds Playhouse opened in 1970 in a building loaned to the Leeds Theatre Trust by the University of Leeds. The first performance was staged on Wednesday 16 September 1970. The photograph shows the Playhouse nearing completion in July 1970.

Leeds Playhouse
The photograph was taken on 29 April 1975.

Majestic, City Square
Newcastle architect, P. J. Stienlet designed the Majestic, with 2,500 seats, for proprietors Leeds Picture Playhouses Ltd in 1922. Featuring marmo terracotta, made by Leeds Fireclay, Burmantofts, it opened at 2.30 p.m. on 5 June of that year. The Lord Mayor, W. Hodgson was in attendance. The first film shown was *Way Down West*. The auditorium featured wall motifs and an enormous plaster frieze. The cinema also had its own Symphony Orchestra and organ. Ownership switched to the Provincial Cinematograph Theatres (PCT) chain in December 1925, and then Gaumont British Theatres in February 1929.

Majestic, City Square

Closure of the Majestic by the Rank Organisation came with *The Good, the Bad and the Ugly* screened, on Thursday 10 July 1969. Top Rank bingo followed for a time until it became a nightclub – the Majestyk (with Jumpin' Jacks in the basement). It was designated a Grade II listed building by English Heritage on 14 June 1993 and a proposal to turn the building into a casino was rejected by Leeds Council in 2009. A major refurbishment programme has since been carried out with the main auditorium converted into retail units.

Paramount, The Headrow

The Lord Mayor of Leeds, Alderman F. B. Simpson, attended the opening of the Paramount at 7 p.m. on Monday 22 February 1932. London architect, Frank T. Verity designed the premises for proprietors Paramount Theatre Ltd. They featured a Portland stone façade and seating was provided for 2,590 patrons. A 17-ton Wurlitzer organ with 2,000 pipes and 160 stops worth £10,000 was also installed. *The Smiling Lieutenant* starring Maurice Chevalier, Claudette Colbert and Miriam Hopkin was the opening film. The photograph was taken in March 1932.

Paramount/Odeon Headrow

On Monday 15 April 1940 the Paramount became the Odeon. The Beatles played there in June 1963, November 1963 and October 1964. The cinema ran two screens from 15 May 1969 and Odeon 3 opened on Sunday 23 July 1978. The cinema was closed on 28 October 2001 and the final films were *Jeepers Creepers*, *American Pie 2*, *Atlantis*, *American Sweethearts*, *The Fast and the Furious* and *Cats and Dogs*. The building, designated a Grade II listing, has since been converted to housing on the upper floor and a Primark clothing store at ground level. The top picture was taken in March 1932 and the one below in September 1946.

Picture House/Rialto, Briggate

Architect Reginald Naylor and George Sale designed the Picture House which was opened on Tuesday afternoon 4 April 1911 by Mrs Curer Briggs the wife of a former Lord Mayor of Leeds. The opening featured *Henry VIII* acted by Sir H. Beerbolm and the entire company from His Majesty's Theatre London. There were 600 seats for patrons along with Wedgewood and Jacobean Tea Lounges and a smoke room. The lessee was Provincial Cinematograph Theatres Ltd and the proprietor John Smith Ltd. The Picture House became the Rialto on 4 February 1927 and closure, with *Woman Teaser*, starring George Raft and Joan Blondell, occurred on 11 March 1939. The building was subsequently demolished and the site occupied by Marks & Spencer.

Pavilion Picture Palace, Dewsbury Road

With 820 seats for patrons, the Pavilion opened its doors on 4 August 1911. G. Frederick Bowman provided the designs for premises which were operated on lease by Thompson & Metcalf from proprietor William Chadwick. The last film shown was *Eye Witness* staring Donald Sinden and Muriel Pavlow on Saturday 29 September 1956. Thereafter the building was occupied by Rothwell Upholstery Pavilion Store but is presently a Surestart Centre and a Halifax Bank. The picture was taken on 27 October 1986.

Plaza (formerly Assembly Rooms Concert Hall/ Assembly Rooms Cinema), New Briggate

Designed by George Corson and James Robertson Watson, the Assembly Rooms Concert Hall opened in 1898. Films were shown in the building during the early twentieth century. And, under lease to New Century Pictures, it became Assembly Rooms Cinema, on Monday 15 April 1907. Seating was provided for 1,100 in stalls and circle levels. During 1923 the building was given a totally new Classical style cinema interior. Five years later, the Assembly Rooms Cinema became part of the Gaumont British Theatres circuit and the seating capacity was reduced to 900. On Monday 25 August, 1958, having come under the ownership of the Star Cinema chain, the name was changed to Plaza, lasting until closure on 14 February 1985. By 2007, the Plaza had fallen into disuse, but in recent years has seen extensive renovation work. It also has a Grade II listing. The photograph dates from 15 October 1975.

Scala Theatre, Albion Place, Lands Lane

The Lord Mayor of Leeds, William Hodgson opened the Scala at 1.30 p.m. on Monday 24 June 1922. Architects Essex and Goodman produced the designs for proprietor Sol Levy's, Scala Leeds Ltd. Seating was provided for 1,692 customers and the first film shown was *The Game of Life*. The Scala Theatre was taken over by the Denman/Gaumont Theatres chain in March 1928. A Compton 2Manual/6Ranks organ was *in situ* between 1930 and 1954. *Across the Bridge* was the last film shown on Saturday 31 August 1957. The building was converted for use as a furniture store by Waring & Gillow, but in recent times part of it was used by the Costa Coffee chain. Currently the auditorium is occupied by a Miss Selfridge store. The photograph was taken on 18 May 1957.

Shaftesbury Cinema, York Road

The Shaftesbury opened its doors on Saturday 20 October 1928, showing *Beau Geste*. Seating 1,603, this was another one of J. P. Crawford's designs, and it was erected for proprietor, J. E. Anderton. Closure came on Saturday 28 June 1975 with *Death Wish* and *Bad Company*. The building was demolished in July 1980. The photograph dates from 3 March 1978.

Star Super Cinema, Glenthorpe Crescent, York Road

Lost Horizon, starring Ronald Colman, opened the cinema at 6.30 p.m. on Monday 21 February 1938. Architect James Brodie had produced designs for proprietors Goldstones Cinemas Ltd, and the building accommodated 1,286 (ground floor with 870 seats and a gallery with 416). The cinema replaced the Victoria Cinema which formerly existed on part of the site. *Secret Ways* and *Posse* were the last films shown on Saturday 4 November 1961. Bingo followed thereafter, then the building became a snooker hall (Star Snooker) and a social centre. It has since been altered for use as a gym and a martial arts centre.

Above left: **Tatler Film lub (formerly News Theatre/Classic), Queens Hotel Building, City Square**

Formerly titled the News Theatre (opening on Monday 22 August 1938) and Classic (from 4 September 1966) the Tatler Film Club came into being on 17 February 1969. It was renamed Classic on 15 July 1979. The photograph was taken on 29 April 1975.

Above right: **Theatre Royal, King Charles Croft**

Joseph Hobson built the Leeds Casino and Concert Hall during the late 1840s. Around 1856 Hobson extended the Casino into Lands Lane and re-named it the Royal Alhambra. Five years later it was known as the New Amphitheatre and between 1862 and 1864 the name was changed to the Royal Amphitheatre. The Royal Amphitheatre was destroyed by fire in March 1876. It reopened 7 months later under Joseph Hobson as the Theatre Royal. When Francis Laidler took over in 1909, the theatre, in subsequent years, became noted as one of the best for staging pantomimes. When Laidler died in 1957, his wife carried on at the theatre for another 2 years. It was then bought by Schofields, and demolished, the old site now forming part of the Headrow Shopping Centre.

Theatre Royal, King Charles Croft

Scene at the Theatre Royal; the photograph carrying the following information from the *Yorkshire Post* of 1 April 1957: 'On stage ... singing a chorus with the cast of the pantomime *Queen of Hearts* are Margery Manners, Wilfred and Mabel Pickle, and Barney Colehan.'

Tivoli/Hippodrome, King Charles Croft

A theatre on this site dates from January 1849, when a building known as the New Theatre was erected for William Schuking Thorne. The venue was noted for showing straight drama and variety acts. In 1874 it was rebuilt (opening on Christmas Eve), becoming known as the Princess Concert Hall, and subsequently the Princess' Palace. Two further name changes occurred when the premises were titled Tivoli in 1898, and the Hippodrome in 1924, following extensive renovations. Closure came in 1933, the last performance was on 10 June, with Count Berni Vici and his Royal Embassy Band. The building was not demolished until October 1967 having been converted for use as Schofield's workshop and a warehouse in the intervening years.

Tower Picture House, New Briggate

Architect J. P. Crawford produced plans to convert the Grand Arcade (originally built by the New Briggate Arcade Company in 1897) into a picture house for proprietors New Briggate Picture Houses Ltd in 1920. With seating for 1,188, the cinema opened on Monday 12 April of that year, showing *The Kinsmen* starring Chrissie White, James Carew and John McAndrew; a Charlie Chaplin film was also screened. Closure came in 1985 and the building was converted to a nightclub a year later. The bottom picture shows Tower Picture House in 1975.

Wellington Picture House, Wellington Street, Wellington Bridge
There were 693 seats (524 on the ground and 169 in the gallery) in the Wellington Picture House which was designed by G. Fred Bowman for proprietor Max Goldstone. The cinema existed between 9 November 1920 and 5 November 1941. Demolition then followed.

Victoria Picture Hall, Glenthorpe Crescent
Designed by W. C. Rodgers, for proprietor Arthur Bew, the cinema, seating 510, existed between 25 October 1912 and 1937. The premises were then demolished and the site used to accommodate the new Star cinema.

West Yorkshire Playhouse, Playhouse Square, Quarry Hill

The West Yorkshire Playhouse opened in March 1990 as successor to Leeds Playhouse when the latter relocated to the Quarry Hill area of the city as part of a major regeneration scheme. The foundation stone was laid by Dame Judi Dench in 1989, and on completion, at a cost of £13 million, it was opened by Diana Rigg. The building includes two theatres; the Quarry Theatre, seating 750; and the Courtyard Theatre, 350. The theatre's first artistic director was Jude Kelly (1990–2002). The top picture shows the building under construction; the exterior view was taken on 31 December 1991.

Leeds District

Armley – Lyric Picture House, Tong Road
The official opening of the cinema on Thursday 7 December 1922 was attended by the Lord Mayor of Leeds, Alderman F. Fountain, but due to technical difficulties a musical programme was the entertainment for the evening. *The Three Musketeers*, starring Douglas Fairbanks, was the opening film two days later, on Saturday 9 December 1922. Hobson & Walker fronted the venture, the building was designed by Jones & Stocks and seating was provided for 900 patrons. During the 1970s there were several closures and re-openings of the cinema. Copyright photograph reproduced courtesy of Betty Longbottom.

Beeston – Rex Cinema, Gypsy Lane
The grand opening of the Rex at 6.15 p.m. on Monday 13 February 1939 featured *We're Going to Be Rich* with Gracie Fields and Victor McLaglan. The building, seating 1,350, was built by Mathews & Sons to the designs of A. V. Montague for proprietors West Leeds Amusements Ltd. Closure came on Saturday 28 February 1976 with the showing of *Apple Dumpling Gang* and *Sword in the Stone*. Demolition followed and the site was redeveloped for housing.

Armley – Pictureland/Western Talkie/New Western, Branch Road
Converted from a Primitive Methodist Chapel, the Pictureland was opened by proprietors American Bioscope Co. Ltd (later taken over by Tommy Thompson and Charles Metcalf) on Monday 25 April 1910. Seating was provided for 439. The cinema's name was changed to Western Talkie on 9 November 1933 and it closed on Saturday 26 May 1956 only to reopen again as the New Western on 21 October 1957. Final closure came on Friday 30 December 1960, after showing *The Unforgiven* starring Burt Lancaster. The building was subsequently used for bingo and then became an amusement arcade. The photograph dates from 21 October 1986.

Beeston Hill – New Crescent Super Cinema, Dewsbury Road

The New Crescent Super Cinema opened on Bank Holiday Monday, 1 August 1921 with *Build Thy House*, starring Henry Ainley. The building was designed by architects C. C. Chadwick and Wm Watson for proprietors John Claughton and Lionel Harpham. Seating was provided for 1,158 patrons. It housed a single, manual Brindley & Foster Clavorchestra Organ, installed at a cost of £3,000 in 1921. Closure came on Saturday 13 July 1968 with *The Man Outside* featuring Van Heflin. The premises were subsequently used for bingo. The bottom picture was taken on 27 October 1986.

Beeston Hill – Malvern Picture Palace, Beeston Roadl

Paragon Pictures Ltd was responsible for opening the cinema and the first film shown was *A Girl's Bravery* on Monday 23 December 1912. Affording 850 seats for patrons, the premises were built to the designs of architect W. E. Beevers. Closure came on Saturday 28 August 1971 with *Carry on Sergeant* and *Carry On Teacher*. The building was used for a time afterwards as a bingo hall.

Bramley – Clifton Cinema, Stanningley Road

Westfield Pictures (Cansfields) were responsible for building the Clifton Cinema to the designs of Bradford architects William Illingworth & Son. It opened at 6.15 p.m. 30 January 1939 with *Woman Against Woman* and *The Case of the Missing Blonde*. The cinema had seating for 1,300, a 30 feet wide proscenium and was equipped with a Western Electric sound system. Existing for a little over 22 years, the Clifton closed on Saturday 17 June 1961 with *Carry On Regardless* starring Sid James and Liz Frazer. For a time the premises were used a Do-It-Yourself centre – Howarth Forest Products. The building has since been demolished and the site redeveloped.

Burmantofts – Regent Picture House, Torre Road

Designed by Fred Mitchell, the Regent had 1,076 seats for patrons when it opened on Monday 1 May 1916. *Both Sides of Life* was the first film shown by proprietor Thomas Abbot t/a Leeds Picture Houses Ltd. By 1943 the cinema was controlled by Leeds & District Picture Houses, and the seating was reduced to 866. The building was fire damaged in 1960, but *The Bounty Killers* with Yul Brynner was the last film to be seen on Saturday 29 May 1971. Later the building was used as a bingo hall and then by a tile company. Copyright photograph reproduced courtesy of Betty Longbottom.

Burley – Lyceum Picture House, Cardigan Road

The architectural firm of Thomas Winn & Sons designed the Lyceum for proprietor George Weldon and seating was provided for 708 persons. A licence for the cinema was granted on Friday 7 May 1913. Closure came after the showing of *Guess Who's Coming To Dinner* on Saturday 11 May 1968.

Chapel Allerton – Dominion Cinema, Montreal Avenue

There were seats available for 1,486 patrons when the Dominion opened its doors at 6.30 p.m. on Thursday 4 January 1934. Architect Alderman William Illingworth designed the building for proprietors and builders A. Cansfield & Sons. The cinema boasted a façade of white stone, a full theatre stage and dressing rooms at either side. *Cleaning Up* staring George Gee was the first film shown. After showing *The Quiller Memorandum*, with George Segal and Alec Guiness, on Saturday 18 March 1967, the cinema closed. The building was used for bingo for a while, but has since been demolished.

Chapeltown – Forum, Chapeltown Road

With 1,500 seats, the Forum opened at 6.30 p.m. on Monday 26 October 1936. It was designed by P. Robinson and the first film shown was *Colleen*. The Forum had an Lafleur/Hammond electric organ which was replaced in 1946 with a 2m.5u. Christie organ removed from the Capitol Cinema, Tonbridge, Kent. After showing *Salome*, starring Stewart Grainger, on Thursday 24 December 1959, the premises closed and were subsequently demolished.

Cross Gates – Regal Super Cinema
The Regal was built in a record 27 weeks by Kenyon & Co. Ltd to the designs of A. V. Montague for Regal Cinema Ltd. The opening film was *Strike Me Pink* shown on Monday 16 November 1936. There was a large car park with spaces for 400 vehicles. *The Longest Day*, with John Wayne and Richard Burton, was the last film shown on Saturday 11 January 1964. Thereafter, the building was demolished.

Harehills – Gaiety Kinema, Roundhay Road
Leeds architect G. Frederick Bowman was responsible for designing the Gaiety Kinema for proprietors Potternewton Estates Ltd. The formal opening was attended the Lord Mayor of Leeds, Councillor Albert Braithwaite, on Wednesday 2 July 1921. The opening film was *Carnival* and seats were available for 1,046 patrons. Following closure, on Saturday 22 February 1958, with *Woman in a Dressing Gown*, starring Yvonne Mitchell, Anthony Quayle and Sylvia Syms, the premises were subsequently demolished in 1972 and the site redeveloped to accommodate the Gaiety public house. Opening on 7 December 1972, the pub had a short life span as it was later demolished. In 2001 the Archway resource centre for 16-25 year olds was built on the site.

Harehills – Hillcrest Picture Lounge, Harehills Lane
The 1,131-seater Hillcrest Picture Lounge opened on Friday 31 December 1920. It was designed by W. H. Beevers for proprietor Allen Nield and the first film shown was *The Woman thou Gave Us*. Existing for just under forty-three years, closure came on 9 November 1963, the final film being *Courage of Black Beauty*. The building has been demolished.

Headingley – Headingley Picture House/Cottage Road Cinema, Cottage Road
The Headingly came into being from the conversion of a motor garage, owned by a Mr Kirk of Castle Grove, into a cinema and it opened on Monday 29 July 1912. The proprietors were Owen Brooks and George Reginald Smith and seating was available for 590. A take-over by Associated Tower Cinemas Ltd occurred in 1938 and in 1972 the premises were considerably altered, re-opening on Boxing Day with *Diamonds Are Forever*. In 2005 Charles Morris took control and the cinema became part of the Northern Morris group. The picture dates from 15 July 1982 and shows Osman Pickthall (right) outside the cinema, with manager Derek Todd.

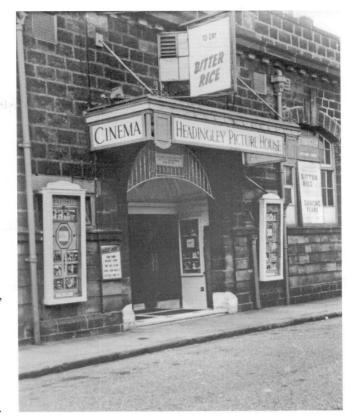

Headingley – Headingley Picture House, Cottage Road

The cinema's website states: 'Since becoming part of the Northern Morris Group the cinema has introduced a special classic film night every 6 weeks. "Classics at the Cottage" has almost become a tradition where patrons can watch the classics in the fitting environment. Recent classic films have included: *Cabaret*, *Casablanca*, *Some Like It Hot*, *The Godfather*, *Breakfast At Tiffany's* and *Top Hat*.' The cinema is pictured here *c.* 1950 and the films advertised are *Bitter Rice* and *Dancing Years*, both released in 1949.

Headingley – Lounge, North Lane

The grand opening of the Lounge at 6.30 p.m. on Monday 2 October 1916 showcased the film *Cynthia in the Wilderness*. The cinema venture was fronted by Mid Yorkshire Entertainments Ltd and architects C. C. Chadwick and William Watson prepared the plans. The building had 782 seats (614 in the stalls and 168 in the circle). The cinema underwent a major refurbishment in 1999 but closed in January 2005 and was demolished, apart from the façade, in January 2012.

Headingley – Hyde Park Picture House, Brudenell Road

The Hyde Park Picture House was formerly a hotel and designs made by Thomas Winn & Sons Ltd converted it to a cinema for proprietors H. and W. Child. The opening film on Saturday 7 November 1914 was *Their Only Son* and seats were available for 587 patrons. The cinema is still in existence and its website states: 'One of the landmark events in the history of the little Picture House happened in 1989 when Leeds City Council stepped in to save it from closure. The Picture House is now owned by Leeds City Council as part of the Leeds Grand Theatre and Opera House Limited.' The photograph dates from March 1976.

Horsforth – Glenroyal, New Road Side

The Glenroyal Cinemas (Shipley) Ltd opened the cinema, with 900 seats, on Monday 1 November 1937. There was a showing of *Michael Strogoff*, starring Anton Walbrook and Margot Grahams on the opening night. *The VIPs*, with Elizabeth Taylor and Richard Burton was the last film shown before closure on Saturday 8 February 1964. The building was subsequently converted to a supermarket. Copyright photograph reproduced courtesy of Andrew Riley.

Kirkstall – Abbey Picture House, Abbey Road

The premises were designed by Fred Mitchell and opened by Messrs Ransley, Dealey & Briggs on Monday 22 September 1913 with *The Web* and *The Ne'er to Return Road*. There were 520 seats (400 tip-up, 120 upholstered) and an orchestral balcony. Music was provided by piano and violin under the direction of W. H. Nettleton. The premises closed on Saturday 8 October 1960 with *Idle on Parade* (with William Bendix) and were used for bingo until the 1980s. The building was subsequently used by a company selling lawnmowers but is presently titled DeLacey House, and occupied by Leeds Mind. The organisation supports people with mental health problems, providing services throughout the Leeds area.

Kirkstall – Imperial Picture House, Kirkstall Road

Proprietors William Ogden and William Fielding were behind the opening of the Imperial on 1 September 1913. It was designed by Leeds architect Arthur Winch and could seat 700. Closure came on Wednesday, 22 May 1940 with *The Girl from Mexico*, starring Lupe Valez, being the last film.

Meanwood – Capitol, Green Road

The Lord Mayor of Leeds, Alderman Frank Fountain, and Revd R. B. McKee, Vicar of Meanwood officiated at the opening of the Capitol on Monday 27 November 1922. The building, which incorporated a picture house, ballroom, billiard room and lock-up shops, was designed by Percy Snowden for owners, The Meanwood Entertainment Syndicate Ltd. The cinema could accommodate 1,294 patrons (1,114 stalls, 180 gallery). *The Prodigal Judge* was the first film shown. Closure came on Saturday 27 July 1968 with *Bonnie and Clyde* and for a time afterwards the cinema became a Mecca bingo hall. Demolition occurred in 1980.

Middleton – Tivoli Cinema, Acre Road

James Brodie designed the 1,152-seater Tivoli for proprietors Golstone Cinemas Ltd. The Lord and Lady Mayoress of Leeds, Mr and Mrs A. E. Wilkinson attended the official opening at 2 p.m. on Monday 21 May 1934. The opening feature film was *A Bedtime Story* with Maurice Chevalier and Baby Leroy. Closure came following the showing of *I Was a Teenage Werewolf* on Sunday 1 May 1960. Copyright photograph reproduced courtesy of Betty Longbottom.

Moortown – Corner House Cinema, Moortown Corner
Pudsey architect James Brodie designed the Corner House and it opened at 6.30 p.m. on Monday 28 November 1938 with 380 seats. The first film was *Yank at Oxford* with Robert Taylor and Vivien Leigh but the venture was short-lived, with closure on 6 January 1940. For a time the building became the Assembly Rooms and was a popular dance venue.

Moortown – Kingsway, Harrogate Road
Seating 1,150 and with a car park for 150 vehicles, the Kingsway was opened by Osbert Peake MP at 7.15 p.m. on Monday 28 June 1937. The designs were prepared by architect James Brodie and the opening film was *Head Over Heels* featuring Jessie Matthews. *Sayonara* starring Marlon Brando was the last film shown on Saturday 23 August 1958. Thereafter, the premises re-opened as New Vilna Synagogue on 6 September 1959. The photograph dates from 22 October 1986.

Morley – New Pavilion Theatre, South Queen Street & High Street

The building opened as a cine-variety theatre in November 1911 with seating for approx. 770. The theatre suffered fire damage in 1913 and by 1916 was showing films full-time. There was a return to full-time theatre in 1929 lasting until 1931. CinemaScope was added in 1956 and closure came on 27 July 1968 after showing *Beach Red* and *Operation Kid*. Thereafter the premises were used for bingo – Star Bingo – and Walker's Bingo – but were subsequently converted to a nightclub.

Morley – Picture House, Queen Street

The cinema opened on 2 February 1914 showing *Dante's Inferno*. Seating was provided for 959 patrons. Closure came on 6 February 1960 after the showing of *The Siege of Pinchgut*.

New Wortley – Plaza Cinema, Wellington Road
Architect James Brodie produced plans for the Plaza for proprietors West Leeds Amusements
Ltd and it opened on Thursday 17 April 1930, showing *Spite Marriage*. Seating was available
for 727. Closure came slightly over seven years later on Monday 28 June 1937. Fire gutted the
building a day later but the shell was eventually used to accommodate a clothing factory.

Pudsey – The Electric Picture Palace and Varieties, Lowtown
Verity's Olympia Skating Rink opened in 1909 but was destroyed by fire in 1910. On Monday
19 December of the same year, a cinema was opened on the site (becoming known as the
Electric Picture Palace and Varieties) in the company of the Mayor and Mayoress, Alderman
and Mrs Forest. *Odongo* was the last film shown at the 'Palace' as it had become known on
Saturday 30 July 1960. The photograph was taken during November 1986.

Pudsey – Picture House, Church Lane
Darby and Joan with Derwent Hall and Ivy Close opened the cinema on Monday 22 November 1920. There were 901 seats for customers. *Doctor in Love* was the last film screened on Saturday 12 November 1960.

Richmond Hill – Princess Cinema, Pontefract Lane
The cinema was opened on Good Friday, 30 March 1923 and J. P. Crawford produced the building's designs for proprietors Cardis and Cohen. *Roustabout*, starring Elvis Presley, was the last film shown on Saturday 31 July 1965. Copyright photograph reproduced courtesy of Betty Longbottom.

Roundhay – Clock Cinema, Roundhay Road

Leeds architect Norman Fowler of Kitson, Parish, Ledgard & Pyman designed the Clock Cinema for controllers West Leeds Amusments and it was built by C. H. F. Lax. The building included a spacious foyer, a café and a parade of shops. At the opening, at 7 p.m. on Monday 21 November 1938, attended by the Lord Mayor of Leeds, Rowland Winn, the first films shown were *The Hurricane* with Dorothy Lamour and Sybil Jason in *The Littlest Diplomat*. The cinema's name was derived from the clock building and there were 1,836 seats (706 circle and 1,130 on the ground floor). A car park accommodated approx. 200 vehicles. After closure on Saturday 28 February 1976 with a Disney double-bill, *Incredible Journey* and *Apple Dumpling Gang*, the building was utilised, first by Mecca Bingo, and then the Empire Electrical superstore. The top photograph dates from 19 December 1987; the one below 6 February 1976.

Roundhay – Picture House, Roundhay Road

Harehills Amusements Co. Ltd commissioned architect W. Peel Schofield to design the Picture House and it opened on Monday 16 December 1912, showing *The Mine Owner*. Seating was available for 900 (700 in the stalls and 200 in the gallery). The *Last Days of Pompeii* closed the cinema on Saturday 5 October 1963. Days later the premises opened as a bingo hall, but were demolished in July 1968. The photograph was taken on 23 July 1968.

Sheepscar – Newtown Picture Palace, Cross Stamford Street

A Cruel Fate opened the cinema on Saturday 11 January 1913. Architect W. Peel Schofield had provided the designs for proprietor W. Hainsworth. There were 788 seats (588 in the stalls and 200 in the balcony). *Captain Blood, Fugitive* was the closing film on Wednesday 2 September 1953. The building was subsequently used as a warehouse. Copyright photograph reproduced courtesy of Betty Longworth.

Stanningley – Pavilion, Stanningley Road

Architect J. P. Crawford was responsible for the designs of the building which he produced for proprietors William and John Harold Hobson. There were 644 seats and the first film shown was *Daddy Long Legs*, starring Mary Pickford, on Saturday 28 February 1920. *Invitation to a Gunfighter* starring Yul Brynner, Janice Rule and George Segal was the last one shown on Saturday 5 April 1970. Afterwards, bingo took hold, and the building was occupied by the Star Bingo and Social Club but, after standing derelict for a while, it has now been renovated and is presently occupied by several businesses. The bottom photograph was taken on 21 September 1988.

Stanningley – Savoy, Bradford Road

The 1,000-seater Savoy came from the designs of William Illingworth for Westfield Pictures Ltd. It opened on Friday 17 September 1937 with *Café Colette* and *Marina Steps Out*. Closure came after the showing of *How the West was Won*, with Gregory Peck and James Stewart, on Saturday 25 September 1965. The building was later converted for bingo. The photograph dates from 21 October 1986.

Yeadon – Picture House, High Street

The premises opened on Monday 3 August 1925 with *The Man Who Came Back* starring George O'Brian and Dorothy MacKaill. Later the building became a bingo hall but was subsequently converted to the Aviator public house.

Wakefield City Centre

Carlton, Grove Road
Ben Firth opened the Carlton on 14 September 1914. It was designed by P. L. Treu and accommodated 1,100 patrons. Later owners included New Century Pictures, Provincial Cinematograph Theatres and the Gaumont British Corporation. After closure on 29 December 1956 the premises were demolished. Photograph from the Tony Moss Collection and reproduced courtesy of the Cinema Theatre Association.

Empire, Kirkgate

Designed by Frank Matcham for the Sherwood family the Empire opened as a variety theatre on 20 December 1909. Besides live theatre, films were also shown as part of the entertainment programme. From 25 July 1921, having been taken over by the New Century Company, the building became the Empire Super Cinema and showed films exclusively. Later owners included Gaumont from 1928. Closure came on 30 July 1960 and the premises were subsequently demolished.

Grand Electric, Westgate

The Corn exchange was built in 1837/8 and the upper floor of the building was converted for use as a cinema, the Electric in 1910, and a year later became the Grand Electric. Later controllers included the Tolfree family. Photograph from the Tony Moss Collection and reproduced courtesy of the Cinema Theatre Association.

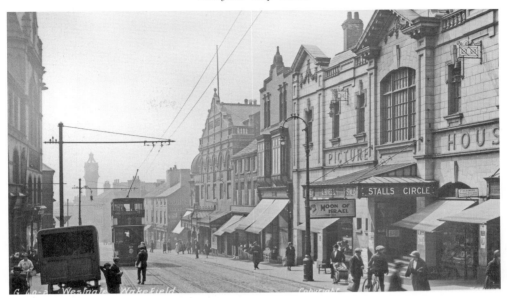

Picture House/Playhouse, Westgate/Prospect Yard

Designed by Manchester architect Albert Winstanley for Sydney Tolfree, the Picture House opened on 22 December 1913 at cost of £13,000. It was Wakefield's first purpose-built cinema and included a small stage, orchestra pit and seated 1,400. In 1915, the name was changed to Playhouse and live theatre also became a part of the entertainment programme. During July 1921 a 3-manual Conacher organ with 2,000 pipes was installed. Later controllers included Essoldo and Classic Cinemas. Part of the cinema was used as a skateboard centre from November 1977, but final closure came in June 1978. Thereafter, it became a nightclub, named Roof Top Gardens, then Quest, and later a pub, Mustang Sally's. The bottom photograph was taken on 17 November 1977.

Regal Cinema/ABC/Cannon

Designed by Associated British Cinemas (ABC) architect William R. Glen, the Regal was opened on 9 December 1935 by the Mayor of Wakefield, Alderman A. Charlesworth. The first films shown were *Gold Diggers* and *Shanghai*. There was a 43 feet wide proscenium, a Western Electric Wide Range sound system, a stage 26 feet deep and seating accommodation for 1,700 (1,100 in the stalls and 600 in the circle). There was also a car park for approx. 200 vehicles. During the 1960s a number of pop stars performed at the venue including Helen Shapiro, Billy Fury, Adam Faith and the Beatles. For a period in the 1960s and 1970s the West Riding Operatic Society put on shows there. Both pictures from the Tony Moss Collection and reproduced courtesy of the Cinema Theatre Association.

Regal Cinema/ABC/Cannon

The last films shown in the single screen auditorium were *Aces High* and *The Best of Benny Hill* on Saturday, 30 October 1976. Three screens were in operation by 11 November 1976 and the following were shown at the re-opening: ABC1 (532 seats), *The Outlaw Josie Wales*; ABC2 (236 seats), *Logan's Run*; ABC3 (181 seats), *Food of the Gods*. ABC was taken over by EMI in January 1969 who in turn were taken over by Thorn in December 1979, becoming Thorn EMI. The latter company became part of the Cannon Cinemas chain in April 1986 and closure of the Regal/ABC came in 1997. The bottom picture was taken on 27 February 2003.

Theatre Royal and Opera House, Drury Lane
The original theatre on this site opened on 7 September 1776 and was built by James Banks for Tate Wilkinson. The theatre opened with a performance of *The Beggar's Opera* and it was usually open for one to three weeks in September, to coincide with Wakefield races. The building could accommodate approx 1,000 patrons. Renowned actress Sarah Siddons performed for one night only at Wakefield on 6 September 6 1786 as Belvedira in *Venice Preserved*. Subsequent owners after Tate Wilkinson's death included Joseph Smedley, Nathan Webster and John Brooke who operated the premises as a Music Hall, known as The Alhambra. In 1883 the premises were acquired by local councillor Benjamin Sherwood and after refurbishment became known as the Royal Opera House. After being refused a licence for a number of reasons in 1892 the theatre closed and the last performance was *False Evidence* on 16 November of the latter year. The building was demolished in March 1894. Distinguished theatre architect Frank Matcham designed a new theatre for Benjamin Sherwood and it was built by F. W. Denholme and Co. at a cost of £13,000. Opening on 15 October 1894, the first performance was the burlesque opera *Brother Pelican*. The picture above shows the original 1776 theatre.

Theatre Royal and Opera House, Drury Lane

For a time in the summer of 1916, films replaced live shows. Subsequent controllers of the theatre after the Sherwoods (Benjamin Sherwood's family had taken control in 1900), included the Gateshead Empire Palace Ltd. During 1954 the theatre was converted to a cinema and opened in the following year as the Essoldo. The first film shown was *The Robe* in CinemaScope. Closure as a cinema occurred on 5 February 1966 and afterwards the building was used by Essoldo (Bingo) Ltd and later Lucky Seven Bingo. On 16 March 1986 the building re-opened after extensive restoration internally and externally for full-time theatre use. A dressing-room block was added at the rear, the stage was reinstated and an orchestra pit excavated. The top picture was taken during October 1982.

Theatre Royal and Opera House, Drury Lane

In 1995 the theatre successfully applied for a Lottery award of £250,000, enabling further refurbishment to take place. Further grant awards came in 2002. On ww.theatreroyalwakefield. co.uk it is stated: 'The event programme at the theatre covers a wide variety of types and style of work including drama, dance, music and comedy. As both a 'producing' and 'receiving' house the theatre generates a growing number of productions with the specific intention of providing particular elements which cannot be sourced elsewhere.' The theatre currently seats 499. The building gained Grade II listing status in 1979.

Trinity Picture House, Belle Vue

Stephen Askew opened the cinema (also known as the Belle Vue Palace, the Palace de Luxe and the Cosy Ciinema) on 7 November 1914 which was designed by P. L. Treu. Control stayed with the Askew family throughout the cinema's existence which ended on 6 September 1960. Afterwards the building found use as a bingo hall, a joinery workshop and is presently occupied by Printforms.

Wakefield District

Castleford – Albion Picture House, corner of Wilson and Albion Street

Providing 600 seats (in stalls and circle) for customers, the Albion opened its doors on 2 December 1912. It was the venture of the Castleford Electric Theatre Company, operated by the father and son partnership of Joseph and Ernest Craven. This building was closed in 1927 and a new one built, a short distance away by the Craven family, opening on 31 January 1927. *The Son of Sheik* was the first film screened there. Subsequent operators included Associated British Cinemas (from 1932), the Star Cinema chain (from November 1957) and Cannon. The building was tripled in size in 1975: screen 1 in the former circle had 350 seats; screens 2 and 3 in the former stalls had 110 and 100 seats. After closure in April 1987 the premises became a nightclub. Copyright photograph of the original Albion reproduced courtesy of Andrew Riley.

Castleford – Queen's Hall, Hippodrome Music Hall/Queen's Theatre of Varieties/Queen's Cinema
A variety theatre, built by the Castleford Concert and Varieties Lecture Hall Company, opened in 1899. From October 1904 it became the Hippodrome and several years later was known as the Queen's Theatre showing films as well as variety on the entertainment programme. It was run as a cinema from 1931 and later operators of the building included the Star Cinema chain from 1942. Closure came on 25 January 1959 after the showing of *The Lone Ranger*. Following a period as an Asda supermarket, the building was razed to the ground in 1990.

Eastmoor – Coliseum/Star Cinema
Designed by W. E. Peters for William Bagnell, the cinema opened in November 1920. Later owners included the Star Cinema chain and Parkrow Cinemas. In line with the changes of ownership, the cinema also took the names Star and Rex and closed on 7 February 1959. Afterwards the building was used as a ballroom, bingo hall and snooker hall.

Fitzwilliam – Plaza Cinema
The Plaza Cinema existed between 1924 and October 1960.

Hemsworth – Hippodrome, Hague Lane
The Hemsworth Hippodrome Company opened the Hippodrome in 1911 and it lasted until
c. 1960.

Knottingley – Palace, Aire Street

Pennington, Hustler & Taylor designed the Palace for the Knottingley Picture Palace Company Ltd and it opened on 25 February 1913. Seating was for 600 people. Later controllers included the R.T.A. Company (John Arthur Rowley, Walter Townend, and Elliot Aspinall) Albert Wilcock, Percy Woodcock and J. M. Scott, Geo. Howdle, A. & D. H. Wood and the Star Cinemas chain. 'Talkies' were first shown at the Palace early in July 1930, the first film being *The Broadway Melody*. Shaun Richardson in his article 'Welcome to the Cheap Seats: Cinemas, Sex and Landscape' published in Industrial Archaeology Review, XXVII: 1, 2005 states: 'The Palace cinema in Knottingley is architecturally and structurally typical of the period. It was built in approximately six months by the 'Knottingley Picture Palace Company Limited'... The building is characterised by an economy of construction – the little architectural detailing that exists is concentrated on the principal road-side elevation while the use of the flanking stair towers and horizontal banding makes the building appear wider than it actually is, partly concealing the bulk of the angled auditorium behind.' The cinema was refurbished in 1953 but closure came on Saturday 3 December 1960 after the showing of *Savage Innocents*. The building was subsequently converted for residential use, with only the façade retained. The top picture dates from 16 October 1989; the one below is a copyright photograph reproduced courtesy of Betty Longbottom.

Lupsett – The Savoy

The Mayor of Wakefield, Alderman Albany Charlesworth opened the Savoy at 8 p.m. on 6 January 1936. Geoffrey Haigh designed the building which held 1,020. The opening programme included the following films: *Going Bye Bye*, *Africa Land of Contrasts*, *Mama's Little Pirate* and *No More Ladies*. Bingo was staged on Sunday and Monday evenings during the months before final closure on 24 February 1962. Later the building was used as a bowling alley and for bingo. Following a fire on 18 May 1963, it was demolished.

Ossett – Palladium, Market Street

The Newtown Picture Palace Company opened the purpose-built cinema on 22 December 1913. The first film shown was *Greater Love Hath No Man* and seating was provided for 800. Closure came on 29 April 1961 and the last film shown was *The Miracle*. Remarkably, the cinema had remained under independent ownership throughout its existence. Just under two years later the building was demolished in March 1962.

1. The New Empire, Moorthorpe.

Moorthorpe – The Empire

Opening in 1912, the Empire featured films and variety on its entertainment programme. Shaun Richardson (*op. cit.*) states that the Empire was converted into a full-time cinema *c.* 1919, '[A]lthough it retained its capacity for live acts and remained the focus of the ambitious local amateur dramatics scene until the 1960s. The only feature to betray the Empire's former theatre origins is the 18m high fly tower at the rear of the building, used to raise or 'fly' scenes and backcloths above the proscenium opening.' In time it became the New Empire and closed on 15 October 1968. Later the building was used for bingo.

Outwood – Outwood Empire

The Outwood Empire opened in 1921 and closed on 1 August 1964. Later the building was used for bingo and as a drive-through fish and chip restaurant.

Pontefract – Crescent Cinema, Ropergate

Built by the Pontefract Cinema Company, to the designs of architects Hustler and Taylor, the Crescent opened on 1 November 1926. Seating accommodation was for 1,200. The building also included a stage, dressing rooms, café and a large dance hall. Later operators included the Star Cinema chain, Canon, Al and Lilian Brook-Smith, Garrick House Cinemas and Facealpha. The Crescent was split for bingo as well as films (becoming known as Studio 1) in 1970 but closure as a cinema came in 1993. Later the building was used by Breaks Snooker Club. The picture was taken during September 1984.

Alexandra, Front Street, Tanshelf
Architects Garside and Pennington designed the Alexandra Theatre for owner Selina Anne
Driver, and it opened on 7 July 1908. Films were included on the entertainment programme
from at least 1909. Conversion to full-time cinema use occurred in 1935. Later controllers
included the Star Cinema chain and closure came in 1961. There was a switch to bingo
afterwards before demolition in 1972.

South Elmsall – Picture House
Designed by architect Percy Archibald Hinchcliffe, the Picture House opened in March 1911 and closed *c.* 1967. Afterwards the building was demolished and the site redeveloped.

Stanley – Stanley Picture House
Designed by architect E. Schofield, for a business consortium, the cinema opened in 1920 with 433 seats for customers. Closure came on 31 December 1960. The building was subsequently converted for use as a petrol station/motor repairs shop.

Bibliography

Holdsworth, Peter *Domes of Delight* (1989)

Hornsey, Brian *Ninety Years of Cinema in Halifax* (2007)

Hornsey, Brian *Ninety Years of Cinema in Huddersfield* (2007)

Hornsey, Brian *Star Cinemas: Britain's leading independent cinema circuit* (2005)

Mellor, G. J. *The Cinemas of Bradford* (1983)

Preedy, Robert E. *Leeds Cinemas* (2005)

Preedy, Robert E. *Leeds Cinemas Remembered* (1980)

Preedy, Robert E *Leeds Cinemas 2* (1982)

Preedy, Robert E. *Leeds Theatres Remembered* (1981)

Smith, Stuart & Hornsey, Brian *Ninety Years of Cinema in Shipley and Baildon* (2003)

Taylor, Kate *Theatres & Cinemas of the Wakefield District* (2007)

Taylor, Kate *50 Years of the ABC Regal Wakefield*

Taylor, C. M. P. *Right Royal Wakefield Theatre 1776-1994* (1995)